12/0 .

D1514882

THE PROBLEM OF VALUE

PHILOSOPHY

Editor

PROFESSOR H. J. PATON
M.A., F.B.A., D.LITT., LL.D.

*Emeritus Professor of Moral Philosophy
in the University of Oxford*

By the same author

*Two Chinese Philosophers: Ch'eng Ming-tao and
Ch'eng Yi-ch'uan*
(Lund Humphries, 1958)

The Book of Lieh-tzǔ
(translation: John Murray, 1961)

THE PROBLEM OF VALUE

A. C. GRAHAM

*Lecturer in Chinese at the
School of Oriental and African Studies
in the University of London*

HUTCHINSON UNIVERSITY LIBRARY

LONDON

HUTCHINSON & CO. (*Publishers*) LTD
178–202 Great Portland Street, London, W.1

London Melbourne Sydney
Auckland Bombay Toronto
Johannesburg New York

★

First published 1961

© A. C. Graham 1961

*This book has been set in Times New Roman type
face. It has been printed in Great Britain by The
Anchor Press, Ltd., in Tiptree, Essex, on Antique
Wove paper and bound by Taylor Garnett Evans
& Co., Ltd., in Watford, Herts*

To

DER PAO

with love

CONTENTS

PART IV: SCIENCE AND MYTH

PREFACE

I wish to express my gratitude to Professor Gilbert Ryle and Professor H. J. Paton for reading the manuscript of this book and making many useful criticisms.

I should like to thank Mr T. S. Eliot and Faber & Faber Ltd for permission to quote from *Morning at the Window*; Mr Ernest Hemingway and Jonathan Cape Ltd for permission to quote from *The Snows of Kilimanjaro*; Mr C. D. Medley and William Heinemann Ltd for permission to quote from *Confessions of a Young Man* by George Moore; Mrs Yeats and Macmillan & Co Ltd for permission to quote from *The Second Coming* by W. B. Yeats; and Mrs Yeats, Shri Purohit Swami and Faber & Faber Ltd for permission to quote from *The Ten Principal Upanishads*.

A.C.G.

PART I

Standards and Judgments

INTRODUCTION

By what standards shall I live? For those of us who cannot accept standards on trust, this question is the one urgent reason for studying philosophy. But there has never been a time when philosophers gave less helpful answers.

The main tendency in recent philosophy, in Britain and America although not on the Continent, is the increasing shift of attention from what language describes to language itself. Before deciding whether a proposition is true or false we need to decide whether it is meaningful; and the new concern with the working of language began with the recognition that this preliminary decision is not as simple as it formerly seemed. The best-known solution of the problem of meaning is still that of the Logical Positivist 'Vienna Circle' of the inter-war period. Its most familiar exposition is A. J. Ayer's *Language, Truth and Logic* (1936), which remains a most stimulating introduction to the problem because of the uncompromising lucidity and directness with which he presented a simple and disturbing case. All propositions are meaningless unless they are either tautologies (such as 'Two and two make four') or are verifiable by sense experience. Since moral and aesthetic pronouncements belong to neither class they are neither true nor false, but meaningless. 'Honesty is a virtue' and 'You ought not to steal' are expressions of approving and disapproving emotions, like 'Hurrah!' and 'Alas!' There can be no fruitful dispute over questions of value except in terms of tastes and goals which the disputants happen to share. Moses blew off his emotions about murder by saying 'Thou shalt not kill'; and if a killer from Auschwitz happens to feel differently, *de gustibus non disputandum.* Philosophy is concerned with meaningful propositions only, and the question 'How shall I live?' is beyond its province.

Pure Logical Positivism is already obsolete. The modern movement inspired by the later teaching of Wittgenstein has taken a direction which seems, at first sight, to restore our confidence in moral and aesthetic judgments. It has finally demolished the preconception, only partly undermined by Logical Positivism, that the main function of language is to describe, and that a meaningful sentence gives a sort of picture of something objective. The Logical Positivists, following the early Wittgenstein, saw that the indicative mood of grammar is no proof that a sentence is descriptive, yet still assumed that the non-descriptive, once recognized, must be ejected from philosophy. But Wittgenstein's posthumous *Philosophical Investigations* (1953) and Gilbert Ryle's *Concept of Mind* (1949) show that language has innumerable functions, referring, describing, narrating, arguing, commanding, deciding, promising, questioning, expressing, exhorting, and that it is useless to draw an arbitrary line between language which belongs to philosophy and language which does not. We talk about real things, certainly, but words about a thing are not connected with it in one simple way as a photograph is; and until we disentangle the functions of the words, they will hinder as well as assist our understanding of the thing.

The assumption is no longer that a sentence is meaningful only if what it says is verifiable by sense experience, but rather that different types of sentence need different tests and that their meaning depends on the kind of test proposed. It no longer seems useful to class moral standards with all other usages which are not descriptive under the single heading 'emotive'. For example, a command is not a description, yet its use is very unlike that of emotive interjections such as 'Hurrah!' and 'Alas!'; moral standards are much nearer in function to the former than to the latter. With this change of viewpoint it becomes possible to admit that moral and aesthetic standards do not say anything true or false either about entities called 'goodness' and 'beauty' or about inclinations and tastes, and yet to hold that they are as meaningful as statements of fact.

But although all this is very reassuring, it must be admitted that Ayer put quite starkly a problem which more recent thinking has obscured rather than solved. Philosophers have never succeeded in proving that moral principles are valid *a priori* in the manner of 'Two and two make four'. They have often tried to deduce moral principles from factual statements about God, social needs, desires, the direction of the evolutionary process; but we have gradually become aware that this is the 'naturalistic fallacy', that we can never make the leap from 'is' to 'ought to be'. Fifty years ago there remained one line of defence for those who held that an action may be wrong however many people approve it—the claim that value is an intrinsic quality accessible to intuition although we cannot prove its presence. But this defence assumes that moral principles are descriptive statements, and is no longer tenable whether we treat them as emotive or as imperative. If my moral principles are commands, and I can appeal neither to reason nor to intuition when I wish to oppose someone who commands otherwise, then they are simply *my* commands. Complete subjectivism which reduces all disputes about value to empty disputes over tastes is not, of course, new: but this is the first time it has seemed inescapable. A modern English philosopher who does try to escape it generally inspires his readers with more respect for his moral character than for his reasoning.

Admittedly there is still a place for reasoning in ethics, as R. M. Hare shows in his *Language of Morals* (1952). But moral prescriptions can be derived only from other moral prescriptions, just as statements of fact can be derived only from other statements. My statements of fact and my moral pronouncements are two independent spheres of discourse; I can pursue internal consistency within each, but they cannot agree or clash with each other. A difference between them is that my factual statements can be verified by observations valid for others as well as myself, so that I can fruitfully criticize another's statements; but my moral standards rest on nothing, so that I can argue with others only when they happen to share the same standards. It will hardly be maintained that commands are independent of the person commanding, and subsist in the upper regions recently vacated by the entities goodness, beauty and truth. My moral standards are *my* commands, which I have the effrontery to address to the entire human race.

I do not accept this conclusion, but I think it can be challenged only with the weapons of linguistic philosophy itself. No doubt it is tempting to deny the consequences of the present revolution in philosophy by denying that it has happened. Why not simply dismiss philosophers so shallow that they see no more in the profoundest questions than confusion in the use of words? But the new preoccupation with language is merely the latest of several advances in self-consciousness from which we cannot hope to retreat to our original innocence. Having assimilated Marx we can never hope, however far we move from Marxism, to unlearn the fact that the interests of classes and other social groups affect beliefs which seem to rest on objective grounds. After Freud, we must recognize that unconscious as well as conscious needs affect such beliefs; and after Wittgenstein, that they are influenced by the structure of language itself. Each discovery of the subjectivity of what seemed objective induces a temporary vertigo, but we soon recover our bearings.

When I discuss the object X, I assume, unless I consciously resist the assumption, that my arrangement of words coincides point by point with the organization of the object. The philosophers of the past were not mere slaves of this preconception, but to a modern reader they generally seem unaware of the degree to which it still affected their thinking. Once I recognize the implications of the fact that a word can have a function without referring to some entity, I am faced with the preliminary question: 'How am I using this word?' If the word is 'house' or 'apple', the preliminary inquiry is soon over; the word is indeed used to refer to a thing, and I can proceed to inquire into houses or apples. But if the word is 'can' or 'want' or 'good', it is disastrous to proceed directly to the discussion of potentiality, desire or value. Such words have functions in types of sentence which do not describe. 'X cannot swim' forbids me to admit, however strong the evidence, that on any particular occasion X swam; 'X wants to go to Athens', in conjunction with other premises ('X has decided to go abroad for a holiday', 'X has enough time and money to go to Athens'), entitles me to infer that X *will* go to Athens; 'Stealing is wrong' forbids me to steal. In each case it may be objected that the explanation of the sentence is inadequate, that there is more, for example, in 'Stealing is wrong' than in the simple imperative 'Don't steal'. But unless the objector can find positive grounds for his conviction that potentiality, desire and value are somehow inherent in the Reality language describes, his reply is merely an invitation to look for a more adequate explanation of the use of the words.

Whether it is reasonable to regret this shift from important-seeming questions about Reality to trivial-seeming questions about words will concern us in the final chapter. Here it is enough to point out that recent philosophers are interested in verbal muddles because these interfere with our understanding of things, not because they prefer words to things. But whether we regret it or not, the revolution is irreversible. If we are to find an objective basis for value judgments, we must discuss them in the terms laid down by linguistic philosophers.

2

HYPOTHETICAL JUDGMENTS

THERE are certain types of sentence which are used not to describe but to prescribe, to bring about actions not yet performed. Among these are commands ('Close the door'), questions ('Why did you close the door?') and decisions '(I will close the door'). In English the first are sometimes distinguished from statements by the imperative in place of the indicative mood, the second by word order; but the last shares the indicative mood and regular word order, and is distinguished from predictive statements only by rules for the use of 'will' and 'shall' which are often disobeyed:

'I will read *War and Peace*. But it is too long. I shall never get to the end of it.'

'I won't give him a penny. But he always knows how to get round me. Probably I shall end up by giving him something.'

Moral and prudential injunctions ('You ought not to steal', 'You ought to be more careful crossing the road') are also commonly in the indicative mood, disguising the fact that they, too, are prescriptive and not descriptive.

An important consequence seems to follow from this—the final refutation of the 'naturalistic fallacy', the illusion that we can deduce moral standards from descriptive premises alone. From statements we cannot deduce commands, questions and other prescriptive sentences, only further statements. This disposes, for example, of psychological theories of value, which try to deduce standards of conduct from generalizations about what men actually want and like.

Now there is a preconception behind this argument which

18

deserves examination. It sharply distinguishes between descriptions and prescriptions, yet assumes that in one important respect they are similar; prescriptions must be justified by inferring them from premises according to the logical rules which govern statements. In the case of moral prescriptions this assumption is quite plausible:

> You ought not to steal.
> To take this wallet is stealing.
> Therefore you ought not to take this wallet.

Yet the point of saying that moral standards are prescriptive and not descriptive is to bring out their resemblance to commands, questions and decisions; and in the latter classes we seldom meet with arguments of this sort. We do, of course, give reasons for such prescriptions, but these reasons are not imperative or interrogative premises from which, when combined with suitable statements, the command or question may be derived. We answer with a *statement* about the purpose of the action of commanding or obeying, asking or answering; we are guilty of the naturalistic fallacy, in the form perpetrated by the authors of psychological theories of values.

> Close the door.
> Why?
> Because I want to get rid of the draught.

Here, to reply with the imperative 'Always close the door while I am in the room', from which the original command seems to be formally deducible, would not in fact answer the question. Again, if I obey the command 'Get out!' and give as my reason 'I didn't want to be thrown out', it would surprise me to be told: 'That is a psychological statement, and the imperative "Get out" cannot be derived from it. You had no reason to leave.'

Since the reasons for commanding, obeying, asking, deciding are reasons for actions, let us begin by distinguishing three ways in which the question 'Why?' may be asked of an action. 'Why did you do it?' is a request for something without which the action would not have been performed; it may be equated with:

A. 'What made you do it?', requesting the cause of an involuntary action. ('Why?'='Caused by what?')

'What made you cry out?' . . . 'I trapped my finger.'

B. 'For what purpose did you do it?', requesting an anticipated effect. ('Why?'='Wanting what?')

'What is your purpose in working so hard?' . . . 'I want to make money.'

C. 'What did you like about doing it?', requesting a quality or part or state of the action. ('Why?'='Liking what?')

'What do you like about smoking?' . . . 'It soothes my nerves.'

When 'Why?' is asked of an expressive or prescriptive utterance, it generally expects the same kinds of answer—not sentences of the same form from which the sentence can be deduced, but a *statement* about the cause or purpose or quality liked. The interjection 'Hurrah!' and the optative 'If only . . .!', to take examples of expressive speech distinguished in English by absence of a main verb, relieve emotion; we can ask the cause of the emotion expressed. They are also used to excite emotion; we can ask the purpose of doing so. Prescriptive speech is a means of making another person do something (command) or tell something (question), or of making oneself do something (decision); it is action to bring about an effect, and we can ask its purpose.

Descriptive speech also is a means of acting on others, and in this case too we can ask the purpose. But descriptive speech is 'about' something, and in addition to the purpose of reporting there are grounds for asserting. I say 'Your box has been put on the train' with the purpose of reassuring the owner, and on the grounds that, according to the porter, 'All the boxes have been put on the train.' A statement may be detached from the purpose of making it in a particular situation, and shown to be entailed by other statements; but it does not follow that we can also take a prescriptive or expressive utterance, abstract the verbal form, and ask significantly whether or not it can be entailed by descriptive statements. There are reasons for expressing a wish to go to Italy, for laughing, for asking someone's name; but there are no premises from which to deduce 'If only I were in Italy!', 'Ha ha' and 'What is your name?'

A statement can be put directly into the 'Why?' form; but in the case of an imperative, interrogative or optative sentence it is only a statement about the command, question or wish which can be put into the 'Why?' form:

Socrates is mortal.	Why is Socrates mortal?	Why are you telling me that Socrates is mortal?
Close the door.		Why are you ordering me to close the door?
What is your name?		Why do you ask my name?
If only I were in Italy!		Why do you wish you were in Italy?

This applies equally to prescriptions in which the verb happens to be grammatically indicative, exposing us to the danger of confusing the prescription with a statement about it:

You are to stay. Why am I to stay? (Why are you ordering me to stay?)
I will stay. Why will you stay? (Why have you decided to stay?)

In practice we do not justify one non-indicative sentence by giving another, and it is indeed grammatically impossible to govern them by such logical words as 'if', 'why?' and 'because'. Admittedly it is possible in theory to construct syllogisms out of non-indicative sentences which look like those of traditional logic:

Let all the guests eat as much as they like.	What are the names of all the guests?

He is one of the guests.

Therefore let him eat as much as he likes.

To hell with all the guests!

He is one of the guests.

Therefore to hell with him!

He is one of the guests.

Therefore what is his name?

I will be polite to all the guests.

He is one of the guests.

Therefore I will be polite to him.

> May all the guests get home safely!
> He is one of the guests,
> Therefore may he get home safely!

But if these are compared with

> All men are mortal.
> Socrates is a man.
> Therefore Socrates is mortal,

it is clear that while in this case we may ask 'On what grounds is it concluded that Socrates is mortal?', there are no similar questions which may be answered by giving the premises of the other syllogisms. In practice such arguments would take some such form as this:

'What makes you think he is allowing me to eat as much as I like?' . . . 'He is allowing all the guests to eat as much as they like (and you are one of the guests).'

'What makes you think he will ask my name?' . . . 'He is asking the names of all the guests.'

Compare:

'What makes you think he holds that Socrates is mortal?' . . . 'He said that all men are mortal (and Socrates is a man).'

The last argument has nothing to do with the truth of the claim that 'All men are mortal'; it merely establishes that the speaker does claim this, and would be a sound argument even if it were untrue that all men are mortal. Similarly, the other two arguments do not give reasons for permitting or taking advantage of permission, asking or answering; they merely establish the scope of the permission or inquiry. It is true that such grounds are sometimes given as though they were reasons for action:

'Why has he decided to be polite to me?' . . . 'Because you are one of the guests (and he has decided to be polite to all the guests).'

But here the 'Why?' is still 'For what purpose?', and the reply is sufficient simply because I do not need to be told his purpose in being polite to the guests. If the reply had been 'Because you were born on January 17', it would merely make me curious about his purpose in being polite to all people born on this date.

The position becomes still clearer when we consider emotive words which are barely within the borders of speech. Thus the reason for shouting 'Hurrah!' is the cause of my enthusiasm or the purpose of making my enthusiasm known. If I give such reasons for cheering, no one will object: 'That is the naturalistic fallacy. "Hurrah!" cannot be entailed by any descriptive statement about cause and purpose.' The word is not susceptible to logical treatment; we can say 'If he cheered . . .' but not 'If hurrah . . .', just as we can say 'If he smiled . . .' but cannot join the 'if' to the smile itself. (Unlike smiling, cheering, being a vocal activity, can be included in speech, like real hair on a wax effigy.) Yet we can construct artificial syllogisms containing it:

> Hurrah for the Glamorgan team!
> Evans is a member of the Glamorgan team.
> Therefore hurrah for Evans!

In practice the argument would be something like:

'Why are you cheering Evans?' . . . 'Because he is in the Glamorgan team (and I cheer members of this team whenever I see them).'

This answer merely calls for a new question, 'Why do you cheer them?' The answer to that would be a statement about the cause of enthusiasm, some victory of Glamorgan, or the purpose of cheering, to encourage the team. There is no need to regret the failure of philosophers to discover an *a priori* categorical cheer which, when combined with empirical hypotheses about the team, would logically justify the cheers of its supporters.

How do moral and prudential advice, using such words as 'ought', 'right' and 'good', compare with the types of prescription so far discussed? The special problems presented by moral advice will concern us later. Here we shall deal only with prudential sentences, which are, it must be remembered, just as much unverifiable by sense experience—for Logical Positivists just as meaningless and emotive—as moral prescriptions are. 'You ought to eat more regular meals' is grammatically indicative, tempting us to mistake it for a descriptive statement. But the grammatical form also exposes us to a less publicized danger, that of assuming that a sentence containing 'ought', 'right' or 'good' remains prescriptive through all the transformations of the indicative mood. Thus it is natural to assume that, if 'You ought to eat regular meals' is prescriptive, then 'Why ought I?' expects a prescriptive answer ('Because you ought to take care of your health'), which itself can be justified only on grounds which include a further prescription, involving us in an infinite regress. But we have seen that it is not prescriptions, but statements about them, which are put in the 'Why?' form, a fact which is obvious when the grammatical form is imperative. The question 'Why ought I to eat regular meals?' is equivalent to:

'For what purpose (wanting what) do you unreservedly advise me to eat regular meals?'

The kind of answer expected is:

'You don't want to ruin your health.'

The answer 'Because you ought to take care of your health' is not logically more satisfactory. It would do in practice, because the man no doubt does want to keep his health; but logically it merely throws the question one stage further back:

'For what purpose do you advise me to take care of my health?' . . . 'There are all sorts of things you want to do which bad health will prevent you doing.'

Advice, like commanding, often uses the imperative mood. The difference between them is that a command is justified by a means and an end of the speaker, advice by a means and an end of the hearer:

Close the door.	Close the door.
Why are you ordering me to close it?	Why do you advise me to close it?
Because I want to get rid of the draught (and closing it is a means of doing so).	Because it will get rid of the draught (an end which you want).

From this another difference follows. The formula for justifying a command is:

I want X.
Y is a means to X.
Therefore do Y.

But there may be many means of achieving X, and many grounds for choosing between them. This does not affect the reasonableness of a command; 'Y is a means to what I want' is an adequate reason for commanding someone to do Y, since it is for the speaker to choose the means. On the other hand, 'Y is a means to what you want' does not entitle the speaker to *advise* someone to do Y; indeed, it obliges him to permit the hearer to choose between Y and other available means. Again, one means may be more or less effective than another, effectiveness depending on whether the hearer wants a quick or a sure means, a thorough or a labour-saving means, and so forth; in this case, the speaker can only recommend one course of action rather than another. To advise, we therefore need more complex forms of instruction than the simple 'Do' and 'Don't':

You want X.
Y is the only means to X.

Therefore you ought to (have to, should, must) do Y.

You want X.
Y is a more effective means to X than Z is.

Therefore it is better for you to do Y than to do Z.

You want X.
Y is an effective means to X, Z is not.
Therefore, of these alternative courses, Y is right and Z is wrong.

You want X.
Y is a means to X.
Therefore you might do Y.

You want X.
Y will not prevent X.
Therefore you may do Y.

But when these distinctions are clear from the reasons given, the simple imperative is not misleading:

'There is no bus which will get you there by 12, so if you want to be there on time take a taxi (you must, ought to, take a taxi).'

'The buses are all crowded at this time of day, so take a taxi (you had better take a taxi).'

Ends are justified by further ends; but unlike the deduction of prescriptive sentences from prescriptive sentences, this does not involve us in an infinite regress. A man, let us say, decides: 'I will go out.'

'Why have you decided to go out?'
'I want to go to the station.'
'Why?'
'I want to buy a ticket for Scotland.'

'Why?'
'I want to go climbing.'
'Why?'
'Because I like climbing.'

To like or enjoy doing something is to do it for its own sake; wants are justified by likings, but likings need no justification. The questioner may of course continue: 'Why do you like climbing?' But this is not another request for an end; to the extent that the man climbs for a purpose, exercise for example, he does not climb because he enjoys it. The question means 'What do you like about climbing?' It does not request one more reason, without the support of which the original decision to go out is unreasonable. It is simply an inquiry to satisfy the questioner's curiosity about the vagaries of human nature. He may no doubt be looking for evidence that the other does not really enjoy climbing. But unless he can find such evidence, or pick out some error in the means chosen, or show that a trip to Scotland will interfere with something which the other likes more than climbing, he must accept the reasoning.

Advice may be conditional or unconditional.

A. *Conditional*. A advises B: 'If you want to keep your job, be more polite to the boss.' A justifies the advice by showing that impoliteness may cost B his job. Evidence that continued impoliteness alone will cost him his job entitles A to advise: 'If you want to keep your job, you ought to (must, will have to) be more polite.' Evidence that impoliteness will not have this effect by itself, but will turn the scale if B makes a mistake in his work, allows him to advise only: 'You had better be more polite.'

B. *Unconditional*. 'Be more polite to the boss.' A justifies this by showing, not only that rudeness will endanger B's job, but also that B will dislike the effects of losing his job more than he enjoys insulting the boss. Whether B is in fact afraid of the sack does not enter into the question. Even if B does not care about the job, A can give the advice unconditionally if he thinks that B will attach more importance to this job when he appreciates the difficulty of finding another. On the other hand, if B does want to keep the job, A cannot give the advice for this purpose alone if he thinks that B is in a rut and will ultimately be grateful for being forced to change.

Fruitful argument over conditional advice, and over unconditional advice when the hearer accepts its immediate purpose, is a fairly straightforward matter. But to convince someone that he needs what he does not yet want is a rather trickier operation; and my conviction that I know the true interests of another person better than he does is likely to owe as much to my vanity as to observation of his character and situation. There is one complication which deserves mention. To the extent that an experience is strange, we cannot tell whether we shall enjoy it until it happens to us. But unconditional advice assumes neither that the hearer shares the immediate end nor that he *already* enjoys the ultimate end. A advises B, a younger man, to go to Italy, a country for which B has no appetite. A expects that B will enjoy Italy when he gets there; he thinks, for example, that once there B will begin to enjoy painting and architecture, to which he is still indifferent. Another person, who has been to Italy and knows B, may appreciate and be satisfied with his grounds for expecting this. But A can persuade B to go only by appealing to ends which B already enjoys. When advice is based on an estimate of what the hearer will like or dislike in conditions now strange to him, its grounds are necessarily unintelligible to the hearer. Such advice takes up a large part of the duties of fathers, schoolmasters, art critics and mystics; and we go on discovering the grounds of already familiar advice as long as we continue to assimilate new experience.

The examples of advice discussed in this chapter are all 'hypothetical imperatives'. The inconvenient fact that one can infer a hypothetical imperative from purely descriptive premises is well known to critics of the naturalistic fallacy. R. M. Hare makes an interesting attempt to dispose of this difficulty in his *Language of Morals*, a book to which I am greatly indebted. His example is:

Grimbly Hughes is the largest grocer in Oxford.

Therefore if you want to go to the largest grocer in Oxford, go to Grimbly Hughes,

which expands to:

You want to go to the largest grocer in Oxford.
Grimbly Hughes is the largest grocer in Oxford.
Therefore go to Grimbly Hughes.

He concludes that this cannot be a valid argument unless 'You want to go . . .' is itself prescriptive and equivalent to the grammatically imperative 'Go . . .' of the conclusion. To show that it is not descriptive, and that 'want' does not refer to any feeling of desire, Hare observes that the argument might be addressed to a member of a religious order whose principles forbid him to inflame himself with the desire to go to the largest grocer in Oxford.[1]

It is quite true, as Hare notices elsewhere,[2] that 'I want you to do X' may be used as an informal command. But 'You want to do X' is not a command, justified by appealing to moral or prudential standards of my own, but a statement about you, tested, for example, by observing whether you take or avoid opportunities to do X. It is a dispositional statement,[3] and does not necessarily imply that you feel any pangs or cravings. Even in my own case 'I want to do X' does not prescribe: wanting is a fact about me, which precedes the decision 'I will do it', and frustrates my efforts to obey the principle 'It is wrong to do it'. Or again, I may feel all sorts of pangs and cravings to do X, yet find excuses whenever there is a chance to do it, and others may know that I do not really want to do it before I discover the fact myself.

The most obvious test of Hare's explanation is to replace the imperative in the conclusion by a formula which, although prescriptive, is grammatically indicative. As it happens, the indicative forms already discussed will not do for this purpose,

---

[1] *Language of Morals* (1952), 1.3.2.
[2] Op. cit., 1.1.3.
[3] Cf. the Appendix to this chapter.

since, as we have seen, the premises determine whether the conclusion shall enjoin absolutely ('You ought . . .'), recommend ('You had better . . .') or allow ('You may . . .'); 'You want . . .' in the premise might be prescriptive without being replaceable by the 'You ought . . .' of the conclusion. But if I say 'If you want to get a seat, it is advisable to book early', this obviously is not equivalent to 'If it is advisable to get a seat, it is advisable to book early'; you must book early to get a seat at all. Even this construction is possible only because indicative forms confuse prescriptions with statements about prescriptions. It is not merely an accident of English grammar that an imperative verb cannot be governed by 'if'. The act of saying 'Go!' is the command itself; it is only a statement about the command ('If I tell you to go . . .') which can be entertained as a hypothesis.

Hare's mistake, it seems to me, is that he does not examine the question which the premises of his example are designed to answer. As we have seen, the 'Why?' of the question is 'Wanting what?'. But if so, there *must* be a 'want' in the premises, and the case which Hare treats as an anomaly is in fact the rule:

Q. For what purpose (wanting what) am I advised to go to Grimbly Hughes?
A. You want to go to the largest grocer in Oxford.
  Grimbly Hughes is the largest grocer in Oxford.
  Therefore (for that purpose, wanting that) go to Grimbly Hughes.

Appendix: Definitions of 'Want', 'Like' and 'Need'

'He wants X' (to eat his lunch, to go to Paris, the overthrow of the Government, the revival of folk dancing)=
  'He is disposed to perform actions of which X is the anticipated effect (purpose, end, aim, goal); to neglect actions which do not have this effect and avoid those which interfere with it; to be disturbed in various ways (hope, anxiety, dis-

appointment, enthusiasm) by changes in the prospects of achieving X; to ponder over alternative methods of attaining X, to feel pangs and gnawings of desire, to enjoy imagining X achieved, etc.'

'He likes (enjoys) X' (talking, listening to operatic music, getting involved in brawls)=
'He is disposed to do X without taking into account any anticipated effect; to resist being distracted from X to do something else; to feel glows and thrills of pleasure while doing X; to want to do X when he is not doing it, etc.'

'He needs X' (money, a square meal, the ability to love)=
'X is an indispensable means to something he wants.'

The man who wants or likes is disposed to act, think and feel in certain causally interdependent ways which cannot be listed exhaustively. Words such as 'desire' and 'pleasure' confuse some of the feelings to which he is disposed with the dispositions themselves; I therefore avoid using them as far as possible.

The definitions do not imply that 'purpose' and 'end', 'like' and 'enjoy' are used as perfectly synonymous words, only that differences in their use do not affect the argument.

For the procedure of definition, cf. Ryle, *The Concept of Mind*, IV, 6 ('Enjoying and Wanting'), V ('Dispositions and Occurrences').

3

NECESSARY STANDARDS

It is usual to divide descriptive statements into two classes:

A. Empirical propositions ('Lions have four legs', 'Paris is in France'), the truth of which is tested by observation.

B. Necessary propositions ('Quadrupeds have four legs', '2+2=4', 'All bodies are extended'), which are true *a priori*. According to a widespread modern opinion, all these are analytic like 'Quadrupeds have four legs', predicating of the subject what is already implicit in its definition.

Hypothetical principles of conduct, according to the argument of the last chapter, are grounded in statements about the relation of means to end and about the wants and likings of the person concerned. Like empirical propositions, they are tested by observation. Are there also necessary principles of conduct which are correct *a priori*, irrespective of an individual's aims and tastes?

We have already noticed the danger of assuming that descriptive and prescriptive language run on parallel lines. However, there are many prudential standards which, like necessary propositions, are valid *a priori*. For example, we can say 'Face facts' or 'Know thyself' without considering anyone's tastes or inclinations, since judging one's situation realistically and recognizing one's own motives and limitations are preconditions of successful action whatever its end may be. Giving reasons for a decision may be reduced to this formula:

I want X.
Y is a means to X.
Therefore I will do Y.

The purpose of thinking how to act is to reach a correct decision. Therefore when I think according to this formula I want 'I will do Y' to be a correct decision. But its correctness depends on the truth of the two premises. Therefore I ought to take into account any fact which bears on the truth of 'I want X' and 'Y is a means to X'. Further, I do not know whether a fact bears on the truth of the premises unless I know the fact. This justifies the principle: 'It is better to know any fact than to be ignorant of it.'

There are other preconditions of success irrespective of our purpose in acting, for example, courage and patience. A curious feature of the words 'brave' and 'patient' is that they are both descriptive and prescriptive. If we want to convey the information that a man is capable of taking risks when they are necessary to achieve his ends, we call him brave. But besides telling us something about the man, the word commends him. Suppose I happen to disapprove of this characteristic; what am I to call it? If I say he is 'rash' or 'reckless', I imply that the risks he takes are *not* necessary to achieve his ends. The solution to this puzzle is that 'You ought to be capable of taking risks if they are necessary to achieve your ends' is analytic. If you want X, and taking risks is necessary to achieve X, you ought to take risks. The same argument applies to the word 'patient', with 'waiting' in the place of 'taking risks'.

The 'harmony' which philosophers used to commend, the 'integrated personality' which psychologists now preach, are also valuable *a priori*. Let us say that activities harmonize to the extent that they assist each other, are in disharmony to the extent that they interfere with each other. If I want X, Y and Z, preventing their mutual interference is necessary to their achievement; therefore I ought to prevent them interfering with each other. Their mutual assistance is a means to their achievement; therefore the more they assist each other the better. The psychiatrist's patient may object to being transformed from a complex and disorganized person into an integrated personality with perfectly concordant desires for money, women, social approval and very little else. But his reasonable objection is to the reduction of his possibilities. His present disorganization prevents him getting what he wants; he cannot claim that disharmony as such is better than harmony without also claiming that it is a good thing to hinder the success of one's own actions.

Knowledge, courage, harmony are necessary as means irrespective of the end in question. There are also necessary ends, which by definition are wanted and enjoyed; the most general is happiness. It is better to live in hope than to live in fear. This judgment depends, not on the observation that men do in fact prefer hope to fear, but on the definitions of the words 'hope' and 'fear'. If I hope for a certain event, I want it to happen; if I am afraid of it, I do not want it to happen. I cannot react positively to an object, be hopeful or interested or amused, without wanting to approach the object and prolong the reaction; I cannot react negatively, by fear or anxiety or disgust, without wanting to escape the object and end the reaction. Analysis of such terms provides us, not so much with necessary principles as with necessary premises about ends. Thus if I say 'You ought not to worry about it', it is enough for me to show that the event which worries you is unlikely to happen, and that in any case worrying will not help you to escape it; I do not have to prove to you that you prefer not to worry. 'Don't take that job unless you want to be worried to death' may be expanded to:

> You don't like being worried.
> If you take that job you will be very worried.
> Therefore you ought not to take that job.

An objector would not demand empirical evidence for the first premise; he would demand it for the second, or appeal to another end which you will enjoy more than you dislike worry.

It does not follow, of course, that in any circumstances we should try to react positively rather than negatively. I have reason to think that someone intends to cheat me; trusting him will make me his dupe, therefore I ought not to trust him. I dislike being tormented by suspicion, wish to be satisfied one way or the other as soon as possible, but I should dislike the loss if he cheated me even more. But it may be that I am always, other things being equal, more inclined to suspect than to trust. Whether we react positively or negatively is due to internal as well as external factors. Sometimes we may say that a man 'really enjoys making himself miserable', that he 'is never happy unless he has something to worry about'. Freud was so impressed by the strength and universality of the appetites for guilt, fear, pain and self-destruction that in the mythology of *Beyond the Pleasure Principle* he assumed, besides the Life instinct Eros, a Death instinct Thanatos. But even if a person's misery gratifies some hidden need, he cannot say: 'I like to be miserable, you like to be happy. Every man to his taste.' The lust for misery cannot be wholehearted, since if there were no conflicting impulse to escape this state it would not be misery. The man who pursues failure is still disappointed by each failure. The man who is never happy unless he has something to worry about struggles to relieve himself from each worry even though he looks for another as soon as it is gone.

The clumsy expression 'Reacting positively rather than negatively' means more or less what D. H. Lawrence and others have called 'Being on the side of Life rather than of Death'. This principle is not as vague as its invocation of two gigantic and much abused abstractions may suggest. It is generally used to imply that we ought to be disposed, other things being equal, to create rather than destroy, love rather than hate, be confident rather than doubt, trust rather than suspect, hope rather than fear, respect rather than despise, express rather than restrain, be interested rather than bored, enjoy rather than feel guilty, take pleasure in seeing others happy rather than envy them, be open rather than closed to new experience. (The list forces us to anticipate the discussion of morals in the next chapter; so far nothing forbids us to include 'Be cruel rather than pity'.) The justification is also quite straightforward. Unless it has effects which we dislike more than the negative alternative, we ought to choose the positive alternative because it is the more enjoyable, and the capacity to choose it is the capacity for happiness. An objection to the formula 'On the side of Life' is that it applies to persons, or books, or civilizations, not to specific ways of responding to things. It is as though we could not call a man's actions good or bad, but merely judge from them whether the man himself is good or bad. But we all compensate for our capacity to advance in some directions by a tendency to withdraw in others, and Eros and Thanatos are entangled within us as inextricably and in as various combinations as good and evil.

How do hypothetical and necessary principles of conduct compare with empirical and necessary propositions? There is one immediately obvious difference. The validity of a proof of the empirical 'Socrates is mortal' or the necessary '$2+2=4$' is independent of context. Granted that all men are mortal and Socrates is a man, no additional information can upset the conclusion that Socrates is mortal. On the other hand a demonstration that 'You ought to do Y' is always liable to revision in the light of newly proposed ends. In the case of hypothetical advice, it is clear that any argument 'If you want X you ought to do Y' is valid only in relation to the end X; there is always the possibility that you ought not to do Y because to do so will frustrate another end which you want more than X. But the same is true of the standards considered in this chapter, which have nothing in common with Kant's 'categorical imperative'. Granted that a means or end is necessary by definition, it must still be weighed against others which are not. When I say 'If you don't want to be worried to death you ought not to take this job', it is an analytic truth that you do not want to be worried, but not that you dislike worry more than you like the advantages of the job. Something disliked by definition may itself be a means to an enjoyable end; 'If you don't want to be frightened to death, stay away from *Dracula*!' might well appear on an advertisement for the film. Similarly, organizing actions so that they do not interfere with each other, and taking all relevant facts into account, are only two of the factors involved in achieving an end. Any muddle or disharmony hinders success, but sorting it out may not be the most urgent task at a particular moment. Any fact may bear on a future decision, but the chances that it will may be negligible, while knowledge of the fact may itself hinder success. A besieged army which knows that the force sent to relieve it has turned back may lose confidence; if it does not know, it may fight on successfully.

In another respect, however, necessary propositions and necessary principles of conduct are alike. The former tell us nothing except in combination with empirical propositions; philosophers no longer hope to deduce any factual information, even their own existence (*Cogito ergo sum*), solely from *a priori* truths. Similarly, necessary standards do not tell us how to act unless combined with hypothetical advice. 'Face facts' tells us to take account of the facts when deciding, but not how to decide. Courage is necessarily a virtue, but whether an act is brave depends on its purpose; the act is not brave if the man wants to throw his life away. To harmonize, there must be ends to harmonize. Granted that it is better to live in hope than in fear, the objects of hope and fear vary with our likes and wants. The end is always assumed; we cannot deduce it from necessary standards.

But in this case, it may be asked, how am I to choose my ends in the first place? Must I choose in Existentialist anguish, by an arbitrary leap in the dark? Such questions miss the point; what I want, need, like, would like if I knew better are simply facts about me, discovered by self-examination, not deduced from principles. Ends which we choose are always means to further ends which we pursue without having chosen them. I choose to devote my life to the ambition of becoming Prime Minister because I already want power, fame, the removal of social abuses, the restoration of England to its ancient glory. Perhaps I am not aware of wanting the first two, and want the other two less than I think. Then the rightness of my choice, in terms of prudence if not of morals, depends on what I really want, not on the validity of any principles to which I appeal; if in fact the experience of power and fame proves unsatisfying, I shall have chosen wrong.

My tastes and inclinations change; I used to enjoy sweets, now I enjoy tobacco, but there was no choice. They also *develop*; increasing harmony between ends, and their modification in accordance with increasing knowledge and self-knowledge, are by necessary standards changes for the better. But this development, which continues as long as I go on learning, preferably until death, depends on a progressive discovery of new facts, about myself and about my situation. I cannot arbitrarily choose my ends, not because there are standards by which to choose them, but because it is simply a fact that I want something and shall continue to want it even if I strive to obey a standard which forbids me to have it. The introduction of moral considerations, which we have so far ignored, will not alter this conclusion. As a moral agent, I respect the ends of others as well as my own. But the ends of others are what they do in fact want, which it is for me to discover and not to prescribe.

PART II

Morals

4

INTRODUCTION

SO FAR we have left moral considerations out of account, and justified decisions solely in terms of self-interest. Is there any reason why I should not be satisfied with this egoism? Is it possible to find a reason for not doing as I like? We have already noticed many grounds for not doing this or that which I want to do at the moment—because objective facts make success impossible, because to do it will frustrate other ends of mine, because success will not give me the satisfaction I expect. Indeed, there is no need to prove to me that I ought to do what I already want to do; every 'ought' marks the advice to do what I shall not want to do until its purpose is made plain to me. However, in all these cases my reason for self-control is that doing as I like will ultimately harm my own interests.

Suppose that I want to steal. Is there any reason why I ought not to steal, which does not come down to these egoistic considerations? There are authorities outside me which condemn and punish theft—society, God perhaps. But I obey the authority either for the egoistic reason that I do not want to be punished, or because I *ought* to obey it, in which case the problem is only pushed one stage further back. What can you tell me about God which proves that I ought to obey Him? That He created me and can destroy me, will reward me with heaven or punish me with hell? Excellent reasons, but purely egoistic ones. That He is 'good', by the non-moral standards so far established? But these cannot provide moral reasons for obeying Him, any more than respect for the qualities of an enemy general can provide moral reasons for surrendering to him. That He wishes only to benefit His creatures and not to harm them? But this obliges me to obey Him only if I already recognize that to benefit others is good and to harm them bad, in which case I already knew that stealing is wrong. A man who loses his faith in the existence of God often feels that he has lost the grounds on which his morality depends, that he must either find new reasons or reconcile himself to egoism. In fact, there never were any grounds; it is only that a problem which before was merely a puzzle of speculative theology is now practically urgent.

Suppose that I quit looking for reasons why I should not do as I like, and argue that it is in my true interests to promote the happiness of others as well as my own. I am a member of society, not Crusoe on his island; the comforts and luxuries, arts and entertainments of civilized life depend on a complex social organization which it is in my interests to maintain; all the objects of my desire are the products of social co-operation in which it is convenient both to others and to myself that I obey the rules. On this view it would be out of place to feel guilt or repentance if I steal, I should merely regret mistaking my true interests. I treat every man as a tool in the service of my own interests, just as much as the thief does; it happens, however, that I have a truer conception of what those interests are, so that outwardly my conduct is indistinguishable from that of someone who recognizes a moral law independent of interest.

This is the theory which the Utilitarians perfected, and which is concentrated in the good old saw 'Honesty is the best policy'. Apart from being false, it has the disadvantage of depending on unconscious fraud. It is, of course, true that the continuance of social order is in my interests. But if I steal, society will not immediately dissolve in anarchy. I injure myself to the minute degree that I contribute to social deterioration; I benefit by the whole of what I steal. No doubt in a well policed society outright theft may not get me very far. Nevertheless, granted that I have the usual egoistic ambitions, money, power and so forth, my best policy will be, not honesty, but striking a mean between that degree of honesty which will put me at a disadvantage in competition and that degree of dishonesty which will involve me with the law, social ostracism or losing the confidence of customers. This assumes an orderly society; in social confusion, of course dishonesty is the best policy.

'Honesty is the best policy' is a proverb which seems designed first to undermine the victim's faith in any morality independent of self-interest and, next, when he sees that it is false, to pitch him into dishonesty. If it does not have this effect in practice, the reason is that those who repeat it wish to be honest from other motives and use this maxim to sustain their will. Similarly the philosopher who equates private and common interests is motivated by a moral passion which is irrational in terms of his own theory. The bourgeois Marxist, rejecting any morally based socialism as Utopianism, persuades himself that since the victory of the workers is a historical necessity it is in his material interests to side with them, although as long as the Revolution can be delayed it is palpably in his interest to defend his bourgeois privileges by resisting it. The Utilitarian, after explaining that the only reason for helping others is that this contributes to my own pleasure, gives me permission to enjoy myself occasionally in order to refresh myself for socially beneficial tasks. Behind the argument for enlightened self-interest one can always sense the philosopher unconsciously conspiring with the reader: 'Neither of us wants naked egoism, and this is the only alternative.'

Among the commonly used arguments against egoism there is a third which does discredit the grounds for preferring egoism to altruism, although it does not provide grounds for preferring altruism. The end of an action is either egoistic, an effect on myself, or altruistic, an effect on someone else. Behaving egoistically, I benefit others in the hope that they will benefit me, or injure them to prevent them injuring me. But I may also want to benefit or injure others without taking account of any effect on myself, out of disinterested love or hate, gratitude or revenge. In the latter case I want the effect on another person just as much as in the former I want the effect on myself; I may want it so vehemently that I may be willing to damage my own interests, even sacrifice my life, for the gratification of love or hate. The absence of grounds for not doing as I want, therefore, has nothing to do with the choice between my egoistic and my altruistic inclinations.

Objectors to this argument have often claimed that the ultimate end of all actions is pleasure, an effect on oneself to which all other effects on oneself and others are merely means. They generally seek to justify morality by showing that helping others is more pleasant than caring for oneself alone, but insist that what is called 'altruism' is merely a subdivision of egoism. 'There are only Epicureans, coarse and sensitive naturally, Christ was the most sensitive.'[1] But it is now widely recognized that pleasure is not the 'end' of most actions, according to any useful definition of the word. Whatever end I pursue, I am pleased if I succeed, sorry if I fail. Anything which I do for its own sake, without any end in view, I enjoy doing. But these two statements do not imply that pleasure is an end; they imply that it is not, since it gives me no further pleasure to achieve pleasure, and I achieve it without having an end in view. Even if we accept the word 'pleasure' at its face value, as referring to a feeling which accompanies certain activities, we must treat it as a by-product, a sign of success, not the goal of action. But in any case this interpretation of the word implies that the claim that we are always pleased by the success of our actions, far from being self-evident, is a reckless generalization, even if we admit the possibility of verifying statements about internal states in one's own case. I may know that I am glad to have succeeded without being able to identify actual stabs or twinges of pleasure. If instead we prefer to take it as a dispositional word, there is no question of regarding pleasure as an end or even a by-product of actions. 'He enjoys doing X' asserts that he is disposed, among other things, to do X for its own sake, not as a means to an end. 'He enjoys helping people' does not assert that helping them tickles him internally in some way, let alone that his purpose in helping them is to excite himself with these feelings. It means that he

[1] '*Es gibt nur Epikureer, und zwar grobe und feine, Christus war der feinste*' (Georg Büchner, *Dantons Tod*).

helps others without taking into account any possible advantage to himself, and without forcing himself in obedience to some rule. The more he enjoys helping people the more unselfish he is.

There is another sense in which it is possible to argue that apparently altruistic inclinations are basically egoistic. It may be claimed that at bottom I want to help others only for the egoistic purpose of avoiding the punishment of society, and that early social conditioning has rooted the impulse so deeply that sometimes I feel compelled to satisfy it even at the cost of my real interests. On this view, morality is not enlightened self-interest and Christ was not the most sensitive Epicurean; the obvious conclusion is that I had better see through the deception practised on me by society, and unlearn any inclinations to help others which endanger my egoistic satisfactions. But the whole argument depends on the false assumption that any effect on others which I seem to pursue for its own sake is socially beneficial. In fact, hatred, revenge, cruelty, the appetite for fame and for power are all altruistic in the sense that their ends are effects on others—to injure, kill or torture gratuitously, to have men repeating my name even after I am dead, to control men for the sake of controlling them, whether they can be useful to me or not. Disinterested hate presents exactly the same problem as disinterested love; the fact that morally we may class it with egoistic desires as bad or potentially bad is beside the point. Indeed, those who insist on the distinction between these two categories are seldom content to condemn both as merely 'bad'. If they believe that an inclination is inherently and not incidentally destructive, that injury to another is its end and not a means of benefiting the agent, they are inclined to condemn it by a special word, 'evil'. The thinker who exposes himself to the lately fashionable charge of lacking a sense of evil is the humanist of the kind dominant from the eighteenth to the beginning of the twentieth century, who explains behaviour in terms either of enlightened and unenlightened self-interest or of self-interest and disinterested benevolence.

Behind the assumption of the primacy of egoism there is

often the preconception that it preceded altruism in the evolutionary process. Granted that we are descended from animals and that the instincts of animals serve their own survival, how can we explain the origin of morality except by a reshuffling of egoistic impulses inherited from our ancestors? But animal behaviour is no more egoistic than it is altruistic. Some kinds of instinctive behaviour have effects which help the individual to survive, other kinds, maternal, sexual and social, have effects which may endanger the individual but help the species. If the maternal instinct appeared as a mutation in a species which left its young unprotected, it would reduce the mother's chances of survival but help her offspring, and therefore presumably be favoured by natural selection. From the point at which man begins to anticipate some of the effects of his actions and use them as reasons for decisions, his newly conceived ends are as likely to be effects on others as effects on himself. It is an unnecessary complication to suppose that he first conceives selfish goals, afterwards aims at the well-being of others when necessary to his own interests, and finally represses his motives in the latter case and comes to regard himself as an altruist.

The necessary standards already proposed authorize us to prefer positive to negative altruism. Loving, we enjoy our reactions to the object and want to prolong and intensify them by approaching and preserving it; hating, we detest our reactions to the object and want to end them by avoiding or destroying it. It is therefore better to love than to hate, and the capacity, other things being equal, to love rather than hate, is part of our capacity for happiness. But so far we have no reasons for preferring positive altruism to an egoism which treats others as means. 'If you want him to enjoy his holiday, you had better not disturb him until he comes back' has the same status as 'If you want him to help you, you had better write to him now'. There are still no grounds for choosing between them except that you want one or the other more.

5

EGOISM AND ALTRUISM

LET us begin with a dialogue between A and B, two characters who have been introduced before, but without giving any biographical information about them. A is the editor of a scandal magazine and is about to print a story about the infidelity of a film star's wife. B is sorry for the husband and tries to dissuade him.

B. But why do you want to print this?

A. It will be good for circulation.

B. But are you sure you ought to print it?

A. Why not?

B. Just put yourself in his place. How would you feel in his place?

A. I am not in his place.

B. But can't you imagine what it must feel like to find a a story about your wife printed in a magazine like this?

A. Yes, I can imagine, but what's that to me? I've got troubles of my own.

B. But he may not know anything about it. Perhaps he trusts her completely. Perhaps he won't know why people are staring at him, whispering, sniggering behind his back. Then someone will post him a copy with the item marked. Why, I should want to shoot myself. . . .

A. Now you're not telling me what he will feel, you're trying to make me feel it. Give me one good *reason* for not printing, or you're wasting my time.

The dialogue thus ends with the victory of A. Nothing that B has said proves that he ought to be kinder; B has worked on

his emotions and failed. There remains the irreducible difference that B cares for the feelings of other people and A does
not. *De gustibus non disputandum.*

But let us look more closely. Both men agree that to decide
A must take into account all the facts of the case, including
how the husband will feel. They agree also that successfully
exciting by rhetoric the husband's emotions in A would alter
the decision to print. But there remains one difference between
them which is not simply a difference of taste. B assumes that
we cannot know how someone feels without sharing his feeling,
A that we can. It is not clear that B has consciously formulated
this preconception, or even that he would be convinced of its
truth if he did; but his case rests on it.

At first sight it may seem obvious that A is right on this
point, yet there are facts that suggest that there may be something in B's presupposition. If B says that A is not an 'understanding' person, or asks him to 'see the husband's point of
view', 'put himself in the husband's place', or accuses him of
being 'imperceptive' or 'insensitive to people's feelings', he
draws no line between knowing about feelings and sharing
them. Is it quite clear that he is using the words ambiguously?
The last exchange between A and B is suggestive in this connection. It is quite true that B does not describe the husband's
emotions, he sets out deliberately to evoke them in A. But in
order to prevent the argument from descending to this
emotional plane, how should he have described them?

Only very simple emotions can be described directly. I feel
sad. Can I put it a little more precisely? Gloomy perhaps?
Listless? Melancholy? A choice between the few available
words does not get me very far. Is it like the mood of a Tchekov
play? Or a Samuel Beckett play? The proposal of these two
unique and complex moods at once shows me that my own
mood is quite different. I can tell you some of the things which
are bound up with this mood; for example, it has something to
do with the bad weather and the dirty plates in the sink,
nothing to do with the falling autumn leaves outside the
window. If I had the literary skill, the rhythm into which my
words fell and my selection and juxtaposition of the features

which affect me would evoke a similar mood in you. Then I
could describe the mood by adding 'That is how I feel'.

But if this is so B's rhetoric is necessary to describe how the
husband will feel. We can excuse him for omitting the formal
'That is how he will feel' at the end; perhaps A's interruption
did not give him time anyway. It seems then that A cannot
understand and accept B's description, cannot know how the
husband will feel, without experiencing emotions which will
shake his decision to print. His position no longer seems im-
pregnable; but before we close in on him, we must examine in
detail what is meant by knowing how another person feels.

For present purposes we may divide the objects of knowledge into three classes: the non-human, ourselves, and other
people. The first class need not delay us; knowledge depends
on sense-perception. We also gain some knowledge about ourselves from seeing parts of our bodies and listening to our
voices, and from the reports of others who see and hear us. I
may not know that I am angry until others point out that I am
denying it at the top of my voice. Generally, however, I do
know that I am angry, without watching myself in a mirror or
listening to my own voice; and, as Ryle shows in *The Concept
of Mind*, there is no need to postulate any introspection by
which I perceive the anger inside myself. The question 'How
do you know Smith is in London?' can be answered: 'Because
I can see him standing over there'. But asking 'How do you
know you are angry?' would be as senseless as asking 'How
do you know you are seeing him?' If my knowledge depends
on perceiving myself seeing Smith and being angry, then my
knowledge of the perception depends on perceiving myself
perceive, and I am involved in an infinite regress. It is true that
I attend to and am conscious of some of my thoughts and
emotions, and this is part at least of what is called introspection. But attention and consciousness, although it may be
easier to say what they are not than what they are, are clearly
very unlike perception; for example, they are a matter of
degree, not like perception of all or nothing. Further, we also
see and hear with varying degrees of consciousness and atten-
tiveness; in this respect also thinking and feeling are on the

D

same level as seeing and hearing, not the objects seen and heard.

When an object is no longer before my eyes I can imagine it. But I do not imagine past emotion; the emotion revives, less vividly perhaps, and mixes with other emotions it excluded at the time. To imagine my fear if the doctor were to tell me I have cancer is to see and hear the doctor in imagination and *be afraid*—a fear which, unlike the real thing, I can of course switch off by ceasing to imagine the doctor. To imagine how I would plan to survive if wrecked on a desert island is to imagine the island and think—not imagine thoughts—about the means of survival.

There is another important difference between my knowledge of other things and of myself. The movements of other things I predict, in terms of cause and effect; my own actions I decide, in terms of means and ends. 'I know what I shall do' implies that I have already decided, not that I foresee. I can, however, predict my involuntary reactions, often in the same way as I predict external events, by objectively applying rules based on past experience of the effect which follows the cause in question. But if the situation is new, I can only think subjectively, imagining the cause and experiencing the effect; I imagine conditions as near as possible to those expected, react to them, and argue from the similarity of the cause to the similarity of the effect. I think of myself on the platform in an hour's time, and my knees shake. Shall I be as nervous when the time comes? If I have spoken in public before there may be reassurance; my nervousness always passes as soon as I open my mouth, the cause does not have this effect. But for the next hour the subjective argument will be the more convincing.

Knowledge of other people, like knowledge of oneself, is both objective and subjective. We see, hear, smell each other as we perceive other things, to a much greater degree than we can perceive our own bodies, and this gives us knowledge about each other which we do not possess about ourselves. Anyone who has watched me for a few minutes from the opposite seat of a railway carriage knows me in some respects better than I know myself. But there is a great deal about me which he could not learn by watching me, and which I would not or could not tell him if he asked. Admittedly, as Ryle shows in *The Concept of Mind*, some of the tendency to postulate unseen happenings inside people is due to logical muddles. 'He knows X', 'He wants X', mean that he is disposed to think, feel and act in certain ways, many of them observable to others, and do not imply unobservable entities called 'knowledge' and 'desire' inside him. Further, there is no need to suppose that thoughts and emotions are different in kind and expressed by speaking, laughing and crying; we can conceive verbal thinking and being angry as processes of which thinking aloud and glaring or clenching one's fists are unnecessary parts which may be voluntarily suspended. But the fact remains that we do voluntarily suspend them, and that it may be both possible and important to get some idea of what a man is secretly thinking and feeling.

My only means to this end is the similarity of others to myself. But this similarity does not enable me to argue immediately from analogy. If two objects are alike, I may infer that they will behave similarly in the same situation. But in this case I am comparing another person to the one thing in the world which I cannot even in principle observe, the one thing the behaviour of which I do not predict but decide, myself. If, then, I am to know what he will do, I must subjectively put myself in his place, imagine his situation, feel as he feels, think as he thinks, decide as he decides.

Putting myself in another's place is not a kind of perception, 'insight', 'intuition', 'seeing into his mind'. The chances are that my re-enactment is very unlike the original, even if it is near enough for the purpose of judging what he will do. In any case it depends entirely on observation of his words, tone of voice, his facial expression and other bodily movements, so that one might be inclined to take it rather as a kind of inference by analogy. But inference by analogy is a separate operation, by which one concludes that the man's situation and personality are in fact similar enough to the model to justify the assumption that he will decide similarly. (Animism amounts to putting oneself in the place of the sun or sea or thunder without checking the utility of the act by this kind of inference.) Putting oneself in another's place is a form of mimicry. The capacity to do what we see done, observe the actions of the only things like ourselves and turn them inside out, goes back to the cradle, to the baby smiling in response to the mother's smile. The actor impersonating a policeman imitates the external mannerisms of a policeman and tries to feel and think as well as talk and walk like one. Insight into another person is similar, but an incipient mimicry not expressed outwardly, like reading silently instead of aloud, or listening to music without stamping your feet.

It is important for the present argument to insist that in putting ourselves in someone else's place we do not perceive, nor infer, nor even imagine his feelings; we try to feel as he feels. A person weak in this capacity is often said to have no imagination; but this is misleading if it is taken to imply that he should be able to form images of another's feelings as objective and separate from himself. I do not imagine another's feelings any more than I do my own in an imaginary situation. Imagining his fear when the doctor told him he had cancer is like anticipating my own if I ever hear the same; I imagine the doctor and feel the fear. When I see someone cut his finger I cannot imagine his pain as something before my 'mind's eye' as his finger is before my physical eye; either I feel a sting like that of the knife's edge and incipiently wince, or I merely see the blade cutting flesh as though it were cutting cheese.

Returning to our snatch of dialogue, before A decides to print his story he *ought* to know as much as possible about both the subjective factors which make him want do this and the objective factors which determine whether the action will have the effects he wants. As we have seen, this 'ought' is *a priori*, and in any case A does not question it. Among the objective factors, he ought to form some conclusions about how the husband will act—whether, for example, he will go to court, or shoot himself, or shoot A. To do this he must, as B points out, think from the husband's point of view. Since he needs to know how much the husband will suffer, he must suffer in the husband's imagined situation. Consciousness of the husband's humiliation and betrayal will clash with his own eagerness to print, in the way that, in imagining a past situation of one's own, recollected joy may clash with present regret that it passed so quickly. From this point 'The husband will not like being publicly betrayed and humiliated' shifts its place from the means of A to his ends; it ceases to be an objective factor which might make it dangerous to print, and becomes a sub-jective factor enforcing the conclusion 'I ought not to print' to be measured against 'I want to increase circulation, there-fore I had better print'. Since the husband will dislike his shame more than A will enjoy the consequences of the slight boost to circulation which a single item will give, A ought not to print.

This is the central argument of this part of the book; let us resume its successive stages. According to the first argument of part I, chapter 3, it is a necessary principle that, when deciding, I ought to take into account any fact which bears on the reasons for my choice. I ought therefore to take into account the aims and circumstances of anyone whom my action will affect. But we have just seen, first, that the understanding of persons is subjective understanding, and, second, that I cannot understand another subjectively without sharing his ends. Therefore I ought to choose in relation to the ends of all affected, not my own ends only.

The whole of this argument seems at first sight open to a very obvious objection. If we have to feel with others in order to know them, should not the overriding practical necessity of understanding the people with whom we deal compel us all to be moral? How is it there are so many successful egoists, people who seem incapable of sympathy with others, yet know very well how to manipulate them for their own ends? To this I answer, in the first place, that the practical need to under-stand others does force us to enter into their feelings; our selfishness is different from, and more dangerous than, a pure philosophical egoism treating all others as means to our own ends, which is an intellectual abstraction of the same order as solipsism. In the second place, the subjective realization of another's needs is not sympathy, it is a precondition of both sympathy and antipathy; far from compelling me to help him, it opens up a new range of possibilities, bad as well as good. The struggle to reconcile the subjectively felt experience of others with our own creates, beside the right alternatives, wrong alternatives—hatred, revenge, cruelty, power-lust, a whole new crop of passions as disinterested as love, gratitude and pity in that they pursue an effect on another as an end in itself, not as a means to any effect on ourselves.

We have seen that such phrases as 'putting yourself in another's place' or 'being sensitive to another's feelings' do not confuse knowing about feelings with having them, since having them is the only source of knowledge. But they do confuse having the feeling with sympathy for it; a cruel person, unlike a callous one, is very sensitive to people's feelings. Returning for the last time to our dialogue, it is far from certain that A refuses to let himself know what the husband will feel, shrinks from an inconvenient impulse of sympathy. His motive may be envy of the husband's success, or enjoyment of the power his magazine gives him over important people, or simply pleasure in making others suffer; in any of these cases he may be imagining the husband's situation as vividly as B is. All that we can know for certain is that he is not being honest with B, and that his air of cool rationality, which at first sight makes such a favourable impression when compared with B's emotionalism, is altogether deceptive. Either he shrinks from imagining the husband's situation or he has unavowed motives; he cannot imagine the husband's feelings before his mind's eye, detached from himself and irrelevant to his decision to print.

We must now abandon philosophy temporarily for psychology—perhaps bad psychology, but its purpose is to illustrate the claim that altruism provides bad alternatives as well as good, not to discover new truths about human nature. As long as I treat another objectively, his actions are impersonal events which assist or frustrate the attainment of my goals; to some I adapt myself, as to changes in the weather, others I further or resist like the growth of plants in my garden or the leaking of water through my roof. But as soon as I begin to respond subjectively he or she is no longer an object which serves me as a means, but a subjective pattern of thinking and feeling, a personality which accords or conflicts with my own. I ask her a question, perhaps, using her as a means to information; it turns out that the question interests both of us; I sense her enthusiasm and enter into it because I share it. Besides the interests common to her and me, I sense in her personality something absent from mine and complementary to it, a vitality which stimulates me out of my habitual inertia, a calm which releases my tense nerves, a grace which soothes my awkwardness, a courage which shakes me out of my timidity. From this point there is the possibility of love or of hate, of the need to approach or to avoid, to realize a personality as vividly as possible or to expel it from consciousness.

To take another example. If my egoistic inclinations conflict I have two alternatives: to find means of reconciling them or to suppress one or the other. Since I want to satisfy both, I ought to prefer the course which enables me to satisfy both; I ought to reconcile when possible and suppress only as a last resort. But perhaps a deep-rooted preference for repressing rather than harmonizing prevents me deciding as I ought; I may be an inhibited or routine-bound person whose first reaction to any impulse which threatens my scheme of life is to suppress it rather than find room for it. The same alternatives present themselves when I feel subjectively the need of another. To the extent that I understood him subjectively I want for him what he wants, and must choose between his ends and mine as I choose between my own, preferring either reconciliation on the one hand or suppression of his or my inclination on the other. But these alternatives are more complex than in the solution of my personal conflicts. The other is an independent agent who acts on motives of his own; reconciling our ends depends on him as well as on me. Seeking to reconcile them I must leap in the dark, helping him, because I want to and not as in egoistic co-operation simply as one side of a bargain, and trusting him to do the same for me. If trust seems too hazardous, if I am tantalized by this liberty which

may at any time, for reasons of his own, draw him into conflict with me, I feel the impulse towards the opposite solution,
to subject him or submit myself to him.

Again, there is the psychological fact that happiness and
unhappiness are enhanced by contrast. I enjoy my holiday all
the more because I have been overworking for months, find
my present poverty all the more bitter because I used to be
able to take comfort for granted. In the same way the contrast
between my poverty and the luxury in which some people live
begins to affect me as soon as I imagine what it must be like to
live in luxury; either I enjoy the day-dream all the more or
envy makes my own condition seem worse. On the other hand,
contrast between another's suffering and my own good fortune
either increases pity or gives a cruel pleasure. Thus sharing
another's feelings generates, together with benevolent impulses,
contrary and equally disinterested impulses to hurt him, envy
and cruelty. Both of these are unstable compounds of his and
my pleasure and pain, since I experience both; envy contains
a pleasant ingredient which constantly tempts me to imagine
over again the scene which torments me; cruelty drives me to
experience as intimately as possible a pain which enhances yet
follows only one step behind the pleasure.

It is often assumed that human behaviour is either egoistic
or constrained by moral principle, but this is an illusion. The
necessity of understanding the people with whom we deal
forces us to 'enter into their minds' and feel subjectively the
tensions between their inclinations and ours; and, as the
psycho-analysts have shown us, self-sacrifice just as much as
self-assertion may be the effect of irrational impulse and not
of moral choice. There is masochism as well as sadism, the
craving to subject oneself to a master as well as the hunger for
power, destructiveness directed against oneself as well as
against others. When both tendencies are present in the same
person quite trivial factors may decide whether his impulse takes
the direction of remorse or of righteous indignation, of suicide
or of murder. What matters to him is to resolve the contradiction between himself and the external world, and he hardly
cares whether he resolves it in favour of one side or of the other.

This kind of fact is puzzling at first sight. It seems natural to suppose that each of us is vividly aware of himself and, even with the best intentions, only dimly aware of others, so that he can never feel the experience of others as intimately as his own, and prefers them to himself only by a moral effort. But a number of factors counter this egocentric tendency. In many circumstances we enjoy putting ourselves in the place of others more than remaining in our own. A simple example is the hero-worshipper, who spends as much time as possible imagining his hero's exciting life and as little as possible conscious of his own dreary existence. Selfless devotion to others is no doubt, as the psycho-analysts claim, often a flight from inner tension, escaping from one's own mind by living as much as possible in the minds of others. Again, we differ greatly both in suggestibility and in the power to suggest. A suggestible person finds it hard to resist the will of a magnetic personality even when it conflicts with his own and is not backed by superior forces; as long as he is physically present the other's ambitions and emotions are more vivid than his own. Above all there is the fact that, however dimly they are present for us, subjectively as well as objectively others have the weight of numbers on their side. For most individuals the respect of others is self-respect, and general disapproval is not only a threat of overwhelming force to which it is prudent to yield, but a proof of being in the wrong.

The selfishness of which we are guilty in practice is an incongruous mixture of egoism with the negative aspect of altruism, a capacity for hatred, cruelty and resentment but not for love, pity and gratitude. A consistent egoism quite unsullied by altruism is a philosophical abstraction. Suppose that I try to act consistently as an egoist, indifferent to any effect on others which is not a means to an effect on myself. Another person is happy or unhappy; I can use his good mood, perhaps, to charm a concession out of him, or take advantage of a time when he is distracted by trouble to steal a march on him; but I shall not be pleased or displeased by emotions which do not touch my interests, I shall be incapable of kindness, pity or cruelty. I shall not be grateful for a benefit, although I may return it in the hope of future benefits; similarly I shall not avenge injuries except as a deterrent to future injuries. I may seek to control him, if he is potentially useful to me; but I shall be betraying my principles if I begin to enjoy the sensation of another resisting and yielding, if I develop a taste for power for its own sake. A good reputation will be merely a means to winning what I want from others; I shall care nothing for the respect or contempt of people who cannot help or harm me, and find no pleasure in the prospect of millions seeing my face on television or reading my books after I am dead. I shall associate with others when they are useful to me, but without feeling either friendliness in their presence or loneliness in their absence. I shall treat my own family in the same way, disregarding the fiction that my children are in some mystical way an extension of myself. Nothing in sex will concern me except the pure physical pleasure; I shall be incapable of love, of Don Juan's pride of conquest, even of caring whether the woman is pleased with or bored by my company. I shall reject all arts and entertainments which depend on participation in the feelings of other people, whether these people are real or imaginary, whether I am watching a game or watching the theatre. All my pleasures will be solitary, even when I happen to be in company; I shall not be exhilarated simply because the people around me are enjoying themselves, nor depressed because they are in low spirits. Clearly all this is not going to be much fun, but my aim is egoism and not hedonism. Successful hedonists are, for short periods, very sensitive to the feelings of those whom with they talk, drink or make love, postpone the question 'Am I getting as much as I am giving?' and do not revert to egoism until the party is over.

This journey towards egoism is not a progressive liberation of the desires from moral restraints, but a step-by-step renunciation of everything we desire except food, raw sex and a few bodily comforts. Its destination is a state near to apathy, emptied of most of the strongest and most dangerous human appetites, and therefore relatively harmless. Admittedly, most of us become egoists in a struggle for mere physical survival—starving men fighting for food, drowning men climbing into an over-weighted boat; but it does not follow that we can be egoists from principle in conditions where basic physical needs are satisfied. The egoist, like the puritan, must inhibit his immediate response in obedience to a principle: 'It is happening to him and not to me. I have no reason to care.' A person who approaches anywhere near this ideal affects us, not as the natural man freed of civilized restraints, but as cold and inhuman, rational to the point of emotional impoverishment. The man who does not use his reason to weed out his emotions is not an egoist; he is selfish and generous, kind and cruel, grateful and revengeful.

Sharing the experience of others is a gigantic extension of the possibilities of happiness and unhappiness. Whether I gain or lose by it is chance; as long as I gain there will be no motive for asking: 'Why let yourself suffer merely because he is suffering?' The question becomes real when, by pressure of circumstances or an inward failure of nerve, I count the cost and expect to lose. Too much of other people's misery tempts me to kill my sensitivity to others and retire inside myself, a retreat which reduces my capacity for happiness and unhappiness alike. When I imagine the prospect of egoism, of being not immoral but amoral, I sense, opposing any moral resistance, a certain attraction, an icy exhilaration at the thought of being detached and self-contained, free from every bond of sympathy, invulnerable to the suffering outside me. This appeal is very unlike the fascination of evil, since the feature which attracts me is not the release of forbidden impulses but the inhibition of impulses which involve me with others and burden me with obligations. It may be urged that I am bound to gain by the retreat, since there is more misery than joy in the world—a generalization on which the best authorities have always agreed, although it is not clear by what standard they judged (their own youthful expectation of happiness?). However, reduced sensitivity will not affect the proportions of joy and misery. Further, on the same argument I gain still more by renouncing egoistic inclinations also and ceasing to feel anything. Emotional frigidity indeed has an attraction very like that of egoism; I shall not be hurt because I shall not care, and a single remaining joy will distinguish my cynical apathy from death, the satisfaction to my vanity of telling myself that I see through all illusions.

A common human type easily mistaken for the pure egoist is the power-seeker. When we think of offenders against the Kantian prescription to treat others as ends and not as means, it is such figures who first come to mind. Since the achievement of power depends on an extensive and thorough knowledge of men, do not such cases refute the claim that it is impossible to understand a man yet treat him solely as a means? Yet there is an obvious contradiction in saying that Napoleon treated other men solely as tools for the achievement of power—over other men. The power-seeker is the man whose supreme pleasure is the sensation of another's will, the stronger the better, tensing itself against his own and snapping. The practical advantages of power are secondary for him; any independent will and unpredictable choice is a threat to his inner security. The remarkable coldness of many power-obsessed men, their detachment from the personal loyalties and grudges which deflect most of us from the single-minded pursuit of a goal, make it easy to confuse them with rational egoists. But they are liable to show the same indifference to the purely egoistic goals, to food, sex and bodily comfort. It is simply that power, like religious salvation, romantic love, scholarly research, and political revolution, is an end which for those who have a taste for it outweighs all others.

6

EGOISM AND SOLIPSISM

THE problem of egoism in morals is very similar to the problem of solipsism in epistemology. It may therefore be useful to examine a parallel version of solipsism and propose a parallel solution. But it is not suggested that the solution will dispose finally of this obstinate and stimulating puzzle.

The solipsist argument, in the form closest to egoism, is: 'I perceive my own mind by introspection, but I cannot perceive yours. Prove to me that you have one.' The egoist argues: 'I serve my own ends, and know no reason for serving yours. Find me one.' Both throw the burden of proof on to their opponents, and all philosophers face the necessity of either refuting or submitting to them. A feature common to both doctrines is that they have a different meaning for each individual. Solipsism means for me that you have no mind, for you that I have no mind. Egoism enjoins me to use you as a tool, you to use me as a tool. It follows that it is illogical to engage in missionary activity for either doctrine. If I convert you to solipsism, the doctrine which your vacant body goes through the motions of professing is false; it is I who have a mind, not you. If I preach egoism, in the first place I gratuitously warn you that I shall murder you should it ever be in my interests to do so, in the second place I work to undermine any prejudices you may have against murdering me. It is therefore natural that no one comes publicly to the defence of solipsism, while professed egoists either irritate us by their air of bravado or disturb us by the implication of unacknowledged motives inconsistent with egoism.

The practical consequences of solipsism and egoism are exactly the same. Conversion to solipsism would not affect the way I expect others to behave; even if they are visions in my mind, they are visions outside my conscious control. But it would abolish my moral obligations to them, in the same way that the denial that animals have minds has been used to exclude them from the range of moral responsibility; the dog may whimper if you beat it, but it does not feel anything. The behaviour of a solipsist would be the same as that of an egoist, who treats others as he treats inanimate objects.

Often one puts down a book on epistemology or ethics with the conviction that the case for solipsism or egoism, as stated by the author before refuting it, is the one watertight argument in the book. Yet believing solipsists are put away, and sane men who profess egoism use the word according to definitions different from ours. Egoism, in the form which shares the apparent invulnerability of solipsism, is the refusal to benefit or injure others except for the sake of effects on oneself. As we have seen, pleasure is not one of these effects; since we are pleased to succeed and sorry to fail whatever our ends may be, the inclusion of pleasure would make it impossible to recommend one course of action rather than another as egoistic. But even with this qualification it might be thought that advocates of the doctrine can be found among philosophers, and still more easily among characters in novels, who are at least evidence of its psychological possibility. Nietzsche evidently will not do, since his whole argument for the amorality of a few is that it develops the superior minority which conventional morality submerges; and Raskolnikov in Dostoievsky's *Crime and Punishment* must be discarded on similar grounds. Even Max Stirner disqualified himself by commending the egoistic pleasure of seeing smiling faces around us. But what about Sade, or, from the same time and place, Valmont in *Les liaisons dangereuses* of Choderlos de Laclos?

No one has ever prosecuted the case for egoism more vigorously than Sade, whose writings are a unique record of a mind at one of the extreme limits of thought and experience:

'Il n'y a aucune proportion raisonnable entre ce qui nous touche, et ce qui touche les autres; nous sentons l'un physiquement, l'autre n'arrive que moralement à nous, et les sensations morales sont trompeuses; il n'y a de vrai que les sensations physiques. . . . Tout individu rempli de force et de vigueur, doué d'une âme énergiquement organisée, qui se préférant, comme il le doit, aux autres, saura peser leurs intérêts dans la balance des siens, se moquer de Dieu et des hommes, braver la mort et mépriser les lois, bien pénétré que c'est à lui seul qu'il doit tout rapporter, sentira que la multitude la plus étendue des lésions sur autrui, dont il ne doit physiquement rien ressentir, ne peut pas se mettre en compensation avec la plus légère des jouissances, achetée par cet assemblage inouï de forfaits.'[1]

This discredits sadism as much as pity; since only physical sensations are real, and we cannot share the physical pain of someone else, it is as irrational to be moved one way as the other. Sade is fond of such self-defeating logic; there is no crime, therefore let us do whatever gives us most pleasure, therefore we should prefer crime since the consciousness of committing it gives an added pleasure: there is no social obligation, therefore all tastes however destructive are permissible, therefore society should make special provision for their satisfaction instead of unjustly favouring the normal. But to press such objections would be to miss the pervading irony of his books. Sade is not an egoist; he wants us, not to treat others as means, but to pursue their pain and destruction as ends in themselves. His egoistic arguments serve only as the first step, to undermine morality before reversing it. Further, he does not want to convince us that we are bound to take the next step, but to tempt us to choose it gratuitously. If his logic were watertight, there would be no choice, and the moral tension would be dissipated. He therefore mixes serious and frivolous arguments, and cultivates an air of dangerous casuistry, in order to strike a mean between convincing and merely disturbing us.

When Valmont, the hero or villain of *Les liaisons dangereuses*, boasts of his victory over Mme de Tourvel, he insists

[1] *Justine* (Le soleil noir, 1950), 48f.

that he does not love her, that he can break with her at will, that he delights only in conquering a strong resistance by a skilful campaign:

'Le surcroît de plaisir que j'ai éprouvé dans mon triomphe, et que je ressens encore, n'est que la douce impression du sentiment de la gloire. Je chéris cette façon de voir, qui me sauve l'humiliation de penser que je puisse dépendre en quelque manière de l'esclave même que je me serois asservie; que je n'ai pas en moi seul la plénitude de mon bonheur; et que la faculté de m'en faire jouir dans toute son énergie, soit réservée à telle ou telle femme, exclusivement à tout autre.'[1]

In the context of the novel this is self-deception, as he half-recognizes; but for present purposes we can take it at its face value. Valmont pursues his own ends in total indifference to the suffering he causes; and it gratifies him that he owes none of his joy to a free act on the woman's part, that he has won it entirely by his own strength, and that he can leave her when he pleases without losing it. According to a common and, of course, perfectly legitimate use of the word, his 'egoism' is gigantic. Yet from our point of view his goal is altruistic, the sensation of Mme de Tourvel fighting and yielding, enjoyed for its own sake and not for any consequent advantage to himself. ('*Ah! Qu'elle se rende, mais qu'elle combatte; que, sans avoir la force de vaincre, elle ait celle de résister; qu'elle savoure à loisir le sentiment de sa foiblesse, et soit contrainte d'avouer sa défaite.... Ce projet est sublime, n'est-ce pas?*')[2] His desire for the applause of his fellows, an essential part of '*la gloire*', is equally disinterested; even when he is mortally wounded in a duel, he is guilty of that ultimate absurdity for an egoist, striking a noble attitude for the sake of an admiring posterity.

Let us criticize a corresponding version of solipsism in the way that we have criticized egoism. The solipsist holds that I perceive my own thoughts and feelings by introspection, and

[1] *Les liaisons dangereuses*, lettre 125.
[2] Op. cit., 23.

imagine (this imagination having the same relation to introspection as visualization has to sight) similar thoughts and
feelings in others; but whereas I can test by observation
whether Venice is as I imagined it, there is no way of testing
whether others have the minds I imagine inside their bodies.
Adapting the argument already used against egoism, we may
object that I do not perceive my anger against the Government
or my thoughts about Nyasaland; I simply get angry with the
Government and think about Nyasaland—consciously of
course, but consciousness is not perception. Similarly I do not
imagine the thoughts and feelings of another, but try to put
myself in his place and think and feel as he does. But in this
case I can neither perceive my own mind nor imagine his, and
the asymmetry on which solipsism depends has disappeared.
Further, even the most ardent critic of Logical Positivism will
hardly find it meaningful to postulate a mind inaccessible, not
only to sense-perception, but to any kind of intuition or
introspection. Consequently, when I try to think from another's
point of view, it is meaningless to ask 'Has he any mind in
which to have such thoughts?'; the only question is 'Is he really
thinking in the same way?' This has a verifiable answer; we
can compare overt speech, and although neurologists cannot
yet compare our silent verbal thinking as nervous processes,
there is the indirect test of my success or failure in anticipating
his behaviour.

Do apes, horses, crocodiles, fish, insects, bacteria have
minds? It seems less and less likely the further we descend the
evolutionary scale. Apparently at some point in evolution
consciousness flickered and a mind lit up inside what began as
a merely physical system. But if so it is impossible in principle
to determine the point. I credit others with minds because of
their physical similarity to myself, and there is no means of
deciding what degree of similarity is necessary to establish the
presence of a mind. However, when I try to conceive the
lighted area inside a cat, I begin to imagine myself seeing in the
dark and moving gracefully and instinctively in a world of
vivid smells. I imagine, not the cat's mind, but the things
outside the cat. The question 'Are these images in its mind?'

E

becomes 'Does it really perceive things like this?', and 'Has it a mind?' becomes 'Is it really possible to imagine things in the way it perceives them?'; and instead of the single undiscoverable point in evolution at which mind suddenly emerged, we have the varying degrees to which a man can 'enter into the minds' of animals, tested by his success in predicting their behaviour.

7

RELATIVISM AND ABSOLUTISM

ARE moral judgments objectively valid? There are a number of possible answers; we shall consider three:

A. Classes of actions are objectively right or wrong irrespective of their ends and circumstances. (Killing a man is inherently wrong even in self-defence; birth control is wrong even if it is the only practical check to over-population.)

B. Particular actions are objectively right or wrong, but must be judged in relation to their ends and circumstances; judgments of classes of actions are merely provisional rules of thumb. (It is generally wrong to take another's property without his consent, but it is right for a starving man to take food.)

C. Particular actions are right or wrong only in relation to the moral code of the person judging; there can be no grounds for preferring one code to another. (You think Hitler was right to gas millions of Jews, I think he was wrong. Let us agree to differ.)

Moral philosophers agree in calling A 'absolutism' and C 'relativism', but which label they stick on B depends on whether the point at issue is the judgment of particular actions or of classes of actions. The present theory of morals belongs to type B; whether the reader prefers to call it absolutist or relativist is his own affair.

A and C agree in assuming that we can judge actions only in relation to standards. But the types of logical justification investigated in this essay entitle us to declare a particular action right or wrong only in relation to the means available in particular circumstances and to the particular ends of the individuals affected by the action. Let us take first a decision of prudence. X has too much work and decides to do without his annual holiday; a little later his health breaks down. If I claim that his decision was wrong, clearly I do not have to insist on the absolute validity of the standard: 'Everyone ought to take an annual holiday.' Equally clearly, I am not reduced to saying merely that the decision was wrong for upholders of this standard, right for anyone who thinks it lazy and extravagant to take a holiday at all. X's decision was objectively wrong in relation to his actual ends; he dispensed with his holiday in order to catch up with his work, and because of the resulting illness he is further than ever from achieving this goal.

Rather than think out every judgment anew in relation to its particular situation, it is convenient to appeal to general principles of conduct, hypothetical and necessary. These principles supply short-cuts to particular judgments, but they do not lead us to any conclusions which we could not reach solely by examining the agent's ends and available means. 'X ought to take a holiday every year' is a hypothetical standard which his present calamity tends to confirm. He wants to keep his health; his present illness adds to the evidence that an annual holiday is necessary to this end. However, the grounds for the judgment that he should have taken his holiday this year remain stronger than the grounds for the generalization to which this judgment lends support; X may still find himself in a situation where the risk involved in stopping work will be greater than the risk of illness. There are also standards of prudence which are necessary, for example the principle that we ought to be brave. But even these do not justify any particular judgment which cannot be derived from propositions about the agent's ends and circumstances. If we review the life of X and find him a coward, we can criticize him on this point without appealing to any standard. He consistently avoided taking risks which, since they were necessary to the achievement of his aims, he ought to have taken. In this case, however, if we find it convenient to generalize the judgment we can do so without any reservation; everyone ought to take risks necessary to the achievement of his aims, courage is necessarily a virtue.

Our inquiry into morals leads to the same conclusion; an action is objectively right or wrong in relation to the ends and circumstances of all affected by it, and we can deduce nothing from moral standards which we cannot discover by analysis of the particular situation. I made an appointment with X and did not warn him that I could not keep it. X does not want to waste his time, and I could have saved him this inconvenience by telephoning in advance; therefore I ought to have telephoned him. My failure to do so was objectively wrong, in relation to the ends of the only person immediately affected. No standard is relevant here, except the basic moral principle that I ought to serve the ends of others as well as my own. However, in the case of morals, reference to a standard is more than a short-cut to particular judgments. Social co-operation depends on common obedience to agreed principles of conduct. In a situation covered by a widely recognized standard, the individuals whom my decision affects, whose ends I must therefore take into account, include all who benefit by or suffer from common obedience to the standard. Let us suppose that X keeps a large sum of money under his mattress, which he does not spend or invest or give away. It does no good to anyone; if it were mine, I should soon put it back into circulation. If I think solely in terms of X's ends and mine, the case for taking his money is very strong. But by disobeying the standard 'Thou shalt not steal', I injure not only X, but all who benefit by general obedience to the standard. Conceivably I might argue that this general obedience is harmful rather than beneficial; I might maintain, with some anarchists, that private theft is a service to society, since it helps to undermine the baleful institution of private property. Even on this assumption I must still take into account all whom the standard affects; I shall steal the money, not only for my own sake, but for the sake of all who suffer from the institutions which bourgeois morality protects.

A moral code consists of both hypothetical and necessary standards. Whether we choose to accept the hypothetical standards is not a matter of subjective taste; they are based on relatively constant and widespread ends and circumstances, in terms of which we can justify or refute or qualify them. Necessary moral standards fall into two classes:

A. Our basic moral rule, that we ought to serve the ends of others as well as our own, entails such necessary principles as that cruelty and envy are wrong. We cannot deduce that homicide and theft are necessarily wrong, since in certain conditions killing may be the only means of saving other lives, the theft of food may be the only means of avoiding starvation. But an action is cruel only if its end is to hurt another, to do something to him *because* he does not want it; cruelty is therefore not only wrong, but the basic moral wrong.

B. Necessary standards of prudence are also necessary standards of morals, since their justification remains the same whether the ends in question are my own or another's. Courage and patience are morally necessary, although they differ from such virtues as honesty and kindness in being preconditions of enterprises of all kinds, selfish and altruistic, creative and destructive. Although the Devil is fully equipped with all vices outside this class, no one accuses him of cowardice, impatience, laziness, weakness of will, an aversion to facing facts.

What men actually want and enjoy is a matter of fact which belongs to psychology and sociology, not to morals. Different individuals and societies have dissimilar needs, and therefore very different moral codes may be equally suited to the ends of those who live by them, equally consistent with fact, free from self-contradiction, and admissible by every necessary standard we can apply to them. We can object to the ends served by a moral code only when they conflict or are unattainable, or when we have reason to deny that the people concerned want them or would want them if they understood themselves and their circumstances better. This last qualification admittedly invites abuse; there is always danger in believing that we know what another man wants better than he knows himself, and it is easy to persuade ourselves that he would share our own ends if he understood himself better. However, if a slave-owner convinces me that his slaves do not want to be free, I am not bound to accept their apparent preference for slavery as final; there is good reason to suppose that they want and would enjoy many things which slavery denies them, and that once they are used to the responsibilities of freedom they will not want to return to slavery. I can insist that they ought to be free without imposing my own ends on the slaves, without assuming that freedom is good for everyone because I like it myself.

Right and wrong change with social evolution and vary with the particular needs of societies and individuals; they are none the less objective. The changing and overlapping moral codes of people, classes, sexes, professions, individuals, never deserve an unquestioning conformity, since they are always in varying degrees imperfect, self-contradictory, dependent on obsolete facts, repressive of old wants for which they have never found room and new ones to which they are not yet adapted, imposing on the weaker the duty of submitting to the ends of the stronger. To the extent that I see through the errors in the code of my own society, and adapt it to my own ends and the ends of those whom my actions affect, I develop a personal variation of the social code, unique since each of us is unique. But this personal morality, like every other, will remain imperfect, always liable to revision in the light of increasing self-knowledge and sensitivity to others, permitting me to decide only on the balance of probabilities, not by the application of certain rules.

According to extreme relativists (type C), we can criticize another moral code only in terms of our own, and there can be no grounds for preferring one code to another. They admit, of course, that there are qualifications to this claim, for example that we can point out contradictions between standards. But if we look closely at these qualifications, we soon find them increasing to the point of ceasing to be exceptions and becoming the rule. Relativism quickly reduces itself to the denial that we can criticize a moral code for serving ends different from our own ends, and shifts its position in our scale from C to B. As an example, let us take the well-known account of the Dobuans of Melanesia in Ruth Benedict's *Patterns of Culture*. The Dobuans believe that no one can gain except by the loss of another, so that a good harvest of yams, for example, depends on spells which entice other people's yams into your own garden; and they are convinced that apparently natural disasters such as disease are always due to the sorcery of enemies. All men are enemies, restrained only by some give-and-take within matrilinear groups, and within larger units in time of war. The most admired personal qualities are skill in trickery, poisoning, and casting spells of blood-curdling malignancy; the ordinary phrase for 'Thank you', we are told, means 'If you now poison me, how should I repay you?' Even husband and wife, as members of different exogamous groups, remain enemies, and when one dies the other is always the first suspect as the murderer; the couple alternates year by year between the wife's village, where she and her relatives bully the husband and force him to work for them, and the husband's village, where the wife receives the same treatment. Although material gain is, apart from sexual prowess, the chief aim in life, each conceals the quantity of his harvest, and quickly exchanges any valuable object which comes into his possession, in order to avoid becoming the target of envy and therefore of murder. This way of life is not a pre-social war of all against all, but a social order embodied in fairly complicated rules and institutions.

We condemn killing for private gain, the Dobuans recommend it; we value conjugal harmony, the Dobuans do not. For an extreme relativist, there is not much more to say. He would admit only that there are a few minor points on which we can criticize the Dobuans without simply ordering them to have the same tastes as ourselves. He would agree, of course, that some of the factual presuppositions of the Dobuan way of life are mistaken. It is not true that one man can gain only at the cost of another, or that disease is the effect of sorcery. He would agree also that the Dobuans would achieve their ends more easily if they resolved certain contradictions in their way of life, if they learned to combine material success with safety and to reconcile the attitudes due to husband or wife as partner in marriage and as member of an enemy group. Moreover, the Dobuans are said to live in perpetual fear, suspicion, anxiety, envy and jealousy. If we point to these as bad features of their way of life, we are not imposing our own values on men who do not share them. There is no need to ask an anthropologist whether the Dobuans agree with us in disliking these states, since they are disliked by definition;[1] a man cannot be afraid or anxious without wanting to remove the cause of fear or anxiety. Finally, a system in which the highest virtues are the qualities needed to injure others is ideally fitted to frustrate the Dobuans whatever their ends may be. This objection does not necessarily depend on the criticism of egoism developed in an earlier chapter. We are discussing the morality not of an individual but of a group, and can judge it only in relation to the ends of the group's members. An egoist might well esteem the Dobuan code, but as his own personal morality. As the morality of the society in which he lives, he would prefer the code which it is convenient to his interests that others should obey. His standards for judging a social code must therefore be the same as a moralist's. The best morality will be that by which all members should help each other, since this will oblige others to help him, while he as an egoist will not help them. It follows that we cannot judge the Dobuan system of conduct as a social morality without requiring it to serve the ends of all Dobuans, and therefore concluding that it ought to forbid one man killing another for his own gain. We cannot judge their marriage system except in terms of the ends of both partners, and must therefore reject customs which encourage each to frustrate the other. But these are the two points at issue on which the extreme relativist agrees to differ.

The present theory of morals is absolutist in its judgment of particular actions. It implies, however, that we cannot pronounce classes of actions right or wrong without taking into account motives and circumstances. Murder, no doubt, is always wrong, but only because we reserve the name for the classes of killing which we consider wrong; self-defence, capital punishment, the just war, the duel, blood revenge, political assassination, the crime of passion, are not murder for those who regard them as legitimate. To except even one of these classes from murder is to admit that the rightness or wrongness of killing a man depends on its motive. Cruelty is

[1] Cf. p. 34.

always wrong, but calling an action cruel asserts its motive. A malicious word which stings for half a minute may be cruel, burning a man at the stake may not. Now a Catholic, for example, holds that such classes of actions as adultery, divorce, pre-marital intercourse, sexual perversion, abortion and birth control are inherently sinful whatever their motives and circumstances, and he will be inclined to call 'relativist' any theory which denies the absolute validity of such prohibitions. The present theory, absolutist by another definition, is undoubtedly relativist by this one. Particular actions are right or wrong; but the kind of action which is wrong when I do it may be right when you do it, the thing which it was wrong for me to do yesterday it may be right for me to do today.

Messrs. A, B, C and D get drunk at a party. A and B have no moral objection to drunkenness, in fact mistrust anyone who is always sober. A drinks seldom, enjoys it when he does, helps others to enjoy themselves, and when he recovers from his hangover returns to work with new energy. B is an alcoholic who is drinking for the first time after giving it up for several months. A is right, B is wrong. C and D both consider drunkenness a sin. C is an inhibited young man who cannot express himself spontaneously and whose rigid but brittle moral principles conceal his envy of those who can. D is a middle-aged man with a deep religious faith of which the sinfulness of drunkenness is an integral part. Getting drunk may improve C, may undermine D; C is right, D is wrong.

When people argue rationally about moral problems, they reason, as they reason in discussions of fact, from necessary principles and factual assertions. (The object of the present book is to clarify and show the logical basis of these principles, not to propose new ones.) Emotional bias and the difficulty of weighing the factual evidence makes it even harder to reach agreement over moral than over factual questions. However, the one event which can make agreement impossible in principle is the introduction into the argument of absolute standards from one of the revealed religions, which at once degrades the decision to an arbitrary and subjective choice.

This assertion will probably seem extraordinary to absolutists and relativists alike. Both assume that, if absolute standards are excluded, the ultimate premises must depend on the subjective choice of the disputant, so that there can be no agreement unless the disputants happen to share common presuppositions. Is it not obvious that since the Renaissance a common religion and morality has dissolved into competing ideologies based in the last resort on the emotional preferences of their believers? I maintain on the contrary that the eighteenth-century *philosophes* were essentially right when they claimed to found morality on Reason. To the extent that post-Christian moralists argue rationally at all, they argue from premises which do not depend on any emotionally determined humanist, liberal or rationalist ideology, but are admitted even by their opponents; it is when they rebel against rationalism as well as against religion, when they begin to search the unconscious and think with their blood, that moral systems become mere reflections of personal taste.

Let us look at a contemporary topic of moral controversy upon which it is exceptionally easy to argue from emotionally conditioned premises, the problem of homosexuality. Those who deny that homosexual practices are morally wrong argue more or less as follows. The homosexual does not choose his preference for his own sex, but discovers it, perhaps after years of refusing to recognize it. His desires are unalterable in the present state of psychiatry, and as urgent as our own desires. Since we ought to aim at the happiness of others as well as our own, we ought to recognize the homosexual's right to act in a way necessary to his happiness, unless there are specific reasons to the contrary. Are there such reasons? Perhaps he may injure others by converting the normal to his own tastes. These tastes are 'perverted' and 'unnatural' in the sense that, physically and probably mentally, men are not equipped to satisfy them as adequately as heterosexual desires, so that even without social disapproval it would be a misfortune to be exclusively homosexual. The homosexual cannot influence normal adults, but may affect the development of adolescents whose sexual tastes are not yet stable. Therefore the homosexual has the right to satisfy his needs with adults of his own sex and inclinations, but should keep away from the immature.

The soundness of this case does not concern us; what matters is the kind of argument used for and against it. The defender argues from a single moral principle, that we ought to aim at the happiness of others as well as our own, combined with factual premises. An objector may question the factual premises and introduce others of his own. Can he also doubt the single moral premise? Clearly he cannot dismiss it as a mere reflection of the defender's subjective taste, as he might perhaps dismiss, should the defender appeal to it, the claim that liberty is inherently good. Even if he refuses to accept it as a necessary standard, he cannot reject it without refusing to discuss the question as a moral issue, in which case all evidence that homosexuality is involuntary or incurable or socially dangerous becomes irrelevant. If he argues from egoistic premises, he can raise no objection if homosexuals injure others to satisfy their own needs, and if people who are physically disgusted by perversion try to suppress it without taking into account the needs of perverts; he must let the two sides fight it out. But as soon as he discusses the question in moral terms, he is committed to deciding it in relation to the ends of both parties.

Is it possible to discuss the problem in moral terms, accept all the factual claims of the defender, and yet reject his conclusions? Only if we can find an additional reason for condemning homosexuality, other than the claim that it injures others—for example, the religious doctrine that homosexual practices are inherently sinful, whether they injure others or not, whether they are necessary to a man's happiness or not. Such a principle outweighs any possible argument which has been, is or ever can be, urged in defence of homosexuality. Its introduction will not be irrational if the theological premises on which it depends are logically demonstrable. But believers in the revealed religions seldom claim more than that their reasons are sufficient to justify a leap of faith from the proven to the unproven. A believer's solution of this and other moral problems depends therefore on his own subjective act of faith, and discards all publicly available grounds of discussion in favour of his own moral intuition. Consequently, he destroys the possibility of arguing from publicly verifiable premises to an agreed solution. The one kind of agreement over premises which remains possible, the kind which to his regret was lost after the Renaissance, is a historical accident, the common acceptance of a religion in a particular civilization at a particular time.

It may be added that although an absolute standard must outweigh all the arguments of the defender of homosexuality it does not reduce their weight. The man who appeals to an absolute standard makes an addition to the defender's premises but does not question them; he fully agrees that we have no right to prevent a man satisfying desires necessary to his happiness unless they are morally wrong, and also that they are morally wrong if they injure others. In the case of desires which are not sinful by his own standards, he would argue in exactly the same way as the defender of homosexuality.

Within the range of actions covered by his standards the absolutist judges with certainty; he can approach the problem of doing his duty undistracted by the problem of discovering what his duty is; he can presume that each man, however stupid and insensitive, is capable of knowing right from wrong. If we reject absolute standards, our decisions become more complicated; we can judge an action only when we know enough about its end and its circumstances, and the validity of our judgments can be probable in varying degrees but never certain. Moral decisions differ from prudential decisions only in respecting the ends of others as well as our own. We choose the most prudent course by weighing probabilities without depending on invariable principles, and we must do the same in morals. We cannot know right from wrong without using factual information derived from self-examination, observation of others, putting ourselves in their places, psychology, sociology; moral sensitivity, like practical cleverness, develops with experience, and varies from one person to the next. And what about the well-known complexity of the human heart, the mystery of human motives? Can we ever know enough about another person, or about ourselves, to value actions at all, if this assumes knowledge of motives? We cannot know enough to be certain, but we have no opportunity to act on absolute certainties anyway. We can be fairly sure that others want food, clothing and shelter and do not want to be killed or robbed, and such relative certainties establish the basis of everyday duties as firmly as we have any right to expect. Less obvious needs present harder problems; but who does find such problems easy?

Absolutists often point out the practical convenience of having indisputable standards, the dangers of the moral anarchy into which we have fallen since they were undermined, the satisfaction of escaping the messiness of relativism and once again making clean deductions from clear-cut moral principles. Such considerations are often presented as though they amounted to a logical demonstration: 'You would much rather there were absolute standards, wouldn't you? Therefore there are absolute standards.' This emotional appeal deserves applause as an amusing piece of roguery, since it contrives to look rational by aiming specifically at the emotions of the rational, their love of order, clarity and certainty. However, from another point of view we must admit the importance of such considerations; they are warnings that we cannot have our cake and eat it, cannot find absolutism baseless without also refusing its consolations.

Is it true that agreement to recognize a system of standards as absolute, even if they are not, is the only defence against anarchy in which everyone believes and acts as he likes? As a matter of history and sociology, social stability seems to be the cause rather than the effect of agreement over standards. During periods of relative stability, men learn to harmonize their ends, or submit them to the ends of stronger social groups according to commonly accepted codes of values; the meta-physical or religious justification of these values, and their claim to absloute authority, have little importance. Social change creates new needs out of accord with accepted values, as well as an altered balance of power, and results in division and conflict between rival moralities. This kind of post-Marxist sociology, in which ends and social groups are no longer conceived primarily in terms of economic interests and economic classes, is as repugnant to absolutists as Marxism itself; they prefer to think of society as a precarious alliance of individuals who cease to fight their natural egoism as soon as they lose their common vision of moral truth. But China, for example, was divided for about two thousand years between Confucianism, Buddhism and Taoism. Among these, Confucianism was a customary code which submitted all standards to the tests of fitness, timeliness, the Golden Mean, while Taoist philosophy explicitly rejected the validity of all fixed standards of conduct. These divisions made little impression on the most stable society in history, and the three doctrines, without ever ceasing to be rivals, assumed different functions within a commonly accepted pattern of life. Imperial China had as coherent a culture as medieval Europe, lasted much longer, and for considerable periods was in much better order, in spite of lacking the supposed benefit of standards commonly accepted as absolute. The two periods in which China was split by fiercely competing philosophies of life are the two periods of rapid social and economic change, the breakdown of feudalism (500–200 B.C.) and the social revolution in the twentieth century.

The morality of Europe in its last period of social stability happened to be absolutist. The constantly accelerating social changes of the last few centuries make it easy to feel some sympathy with the nostalgia of those who are not greatly interested in merely material benefits to humanity. Granted that, as was suggested above, post-Christian moralists do argue from common premises when they argue rationally at all, they cannot in practice reach agreed solutions in a time of social conflict and transformation. For example, it is at least plausible to claim that the profound moral differences between liberalism and Marxism derive from a single question of sociological fact, the Marxist thesis that class interests are irreconcilable, which implies that the moral effort to harmonize my ends with those of others must stop at the limits of my own class. But a final proof that the thesis is true or false or meaningless would have academic interest only, since the two ideologies are identified with opposing interests in a world-wide conflict of classes and nations. In any case we made the proviso 'when they argue rationally at all'; such an important school of post-Christian moralists as the Nazis did not argue rationally at all. Reason cannot, as liberals used to hope, put a new system of accepted values in the place of the old. But religion is as powerless as reason to unify a civilization disrupted by the collision of powerful interests. It cannot even hold on to its own unity under the stress; the Western Church split at the very beginning of the modern world. As long as the accelerating world revolution continues, it will be impossible in practice to agree over moral standards; if it ever comes to a gentle stop, customary morality will no doubt, as it always has done, settle down into an agreed form not quite satisfactory either to reason or to religion.

There is always the temptation to escape from the strain of uncertainty to the inner security of submitting to the only standards conceivable as absolute and universal, those of the particular religion into which one happened to be born. Yet on most of the contemporary moral issues which involve basic differences of principle the absolutist judges on the same balance of probabilities as everyone else, not by certain deductions from eternal standards. Examples are brain-washing, torture, forced labour, treason, anti-semitism, liberty of thought. Until a couple of centuries ago most Christians, in their attitude to such questions, were closer to the Nazis and Communists than to those who seek in Christianity an absolute authority by which to condemn Nazis and Communists. Supporters of Western democracy, whether Christian or not, have exchanged the answers of the Age of Faith for those of Voltaire; the absolutists have changed with the rest, although they were often the ones who changed last.

There is no contemporary moral problem more fundamental than that raised by Chinese 'brain-washing'. We feel that converting another man to one's own opinion, not by persuasion, but by psychological and physical pressure in solitary confinement, is a profound affront to human dignity, different in kind from using force merely to prevent him spreading his opinions. Christians and atheists within the liberal tradition do not quarrel over this issue; we share the same moral conviction, far from self-evident in terms either of Christian dogma or of the moral philosophy of this book, and each in his own way seeks reasons to establish it. The Christian has the advantage that all his moral convictions seem to share the absolute authority of his basic moral principles, however weak the intermediate links. Yet the advantage is no more than a stronger subjective feeling of security, for until a couple of centuries ago few Christians would even have understood what we are talking about. How can it be an affront to your dignity to force you to see the Truth? Will you not realize as soon as you are converted that I have done you a service? Is not the suffering you force me to inflict on you a just punishment for your wicked stubbornness in refusing to see that I am right? It is the absolutist, not the relativist, who must find such questions difficult to answer. Chinese Communist interrogators are not, as is often imagined, amoral scientists who treat the prisoner as a mechanism according to behaviourist principles learned from Pavlov; they are religious men who believe that he is a sinner, one who wilfully refuses to see the Truth and must be taught to recognize his guilt and repent. If an Inquisitor could return to the world and hear how Communists wash the brain clean of the truth, he would swell with righteous anger; but only because Communists are doing to us what we should be doing to them.

Relativism and absolutism appeal for opposite reasons to opposite kinds of temperament. The relativist feels the complexity of all value judgments, the uniqueness of each person and each situation, the impossibility of assimilating judgments in obedience to general principles without debasing them. The absolutist is more impressed by the danger of slipping into a chaos in which value disappears because each person's judgment is accorded equal value. Like all philosophical doctrines which touch the emotions at all, each of the pair appeals to bad motives as well as good. The relativist can escape judgment by refusing to judge others, the absolutist can

F

close his eyes to the possibility that he is doing harm rather than risk the torment of uncertainty.

This is one of the points at which it becomes obvious that temperamental differences between people affect, not only their moral judgments, but their conception of the function of ethics and of the problems with which it deals. In order to bring concealed influences to the surface, it may be interesting to conclude with a table of two opposing sets of preconceptions:

A	B
I need ethics to prove to me that I cannot always do as I want.	I need ethics and aesthetics to assist me in choosing between different inclinations and tastes.
I already know what is right; the difficulty is to do it.	I discover values progressively; to develop standards is as much a problem as to act on them.
Only actions which raise a moral issue have value; the rest are neutral.	All activities are subject to valuation; there is no difference in kind between preferring a generous action to a mean one and choosing between two poems or between a sharp razor-blade and a blunt one.
Happiness is a simple matter of doing as I want; the question is how much happiness I can allow myself.	'How can I be happy?' is one way of stating the problem of values.
A moral choice is between a principle and an inclination.	A moral choice is between a generous and a selfish or destructive inclination.

A generous impulse is worthless unless it is followed in conscious obedience to a principle.

Obedience to a principle is worthless unless it is inspired by a generous impulse.

I judge confidently when I can deduce with certainty from an absolute standard.

I judge confidently when the balance of probabilities is clear; to be certain is to believe that on this point I am infallible.

I develop as the implications of my principles become clearer and as control over my desires becomes easier.

I develop by refining my tastes and desires.

If it is wrong to want something, I develop morally by learning to control the desire; to want it less may be outside my power.

If it is wrong to want something, I develop morally by wanting it less and less; to control the desire is merely useful for society.

To have value an action must be voluntary.

The most valuable activities are at least partly involuntary (love, mystical ecstasy, artistic creation).

I can be certain that an action is right or wrong without knowing anything about the agent.

I can never think it more than probable that an action is right or wrong because I cannot know everything about the agent.

B is a materialist, since he can conceive nothing higher than the gratification of his senses.

A is a materialist, since he can conceive nothing higher than making money except denying himself money to give it to others.

Of course neither of these attitudes is common in a pure state. My own development or degeneration has been from nearer A to nearer B. Score ten out of twelve on the left-hand side, and you may as well throw this book away.

PART III

Aesthetics

8

INTRODUCTION

WHAT is art? What is that unique quality which is shared by *King Lear*, the Katsura Detached Palace in Kyoto and the Goldberg Variations, but is missing from the works which you like and I do not? Is it something called Beauty in the object itself, or is it in the aesthetic response? If it is in the response, what is it that distinguishes the aesthetic experience from all other experiences?

Behind these questions there is a preconception. We say that a work of art is good or bad whether or not everyone can see that it is good or bad; there must, then, be some aesthetic quality which is actually there even if a vulgar person's aesthetic sense is too dim to perceive it. The standards by which we criticize must be statements about this quality. The assumption resembles the preconception that moral standards are statements about qualities inherent in actions and agents, and is open to similar objections.

Where am I to look for this aesthetic quality? Clearly I cannot seek it in *good* works of art, since there is no test of inherent value until I find it. All I can do is look for a common quality in works which I enjoy myself, or—the ordinary method of aestheticians—in some innocuous selection of acknowledged masterpieces which will look rather odd in fifty years' time. The search may reveal interesting facts, such as the frequency of the Golden Section in the proportions of paintings and buildings. But if a common quality does emerge, I can claim only, as a contribution to the psychology or history of taste, that it is common to the works I like or which here and now most people agree in liking. It cannot serve as a proof of inherent value. Suppose that it turns out that at present *all* the architecture I like, and none I dislike, observes the proportions of the Golden Section. Can I henceforth use this formula as a test of good architecture? On the contrary, when next I see a building which satisfies the test, either I like it before working out the proportions, or the generalization about my taste was premature.

A quality can be evidence that a work of art is good only if there are standards which establish that it is a good quality. If, then, we insist on treating critical standards as statements giving us various kinds of information about the aesthetic quality, we are caught in an infinite regress. Let us approach the problem from a different direction. A critic judges symphonies, statues, poems, by applying standards; but he gives unconvincing reasons or none for accepting them as binding, and disagrees violently with other critics over their interpretation and their relative importance. We need to know whether these principles are mere reflections of his personal prejudices or whether they have objective justification. We also need to know when to apply them; and this is the information that we are seeking when we ask the question 'What is art?' We distinguish art from propaganda and entertainment to the extent that we judge it by different standards. If you recommend a book as a serious novel, I have the right to complain that the characters are one-dimensional but not that the plot develops slowly; if you recommend it as a thriller, I shall complain that it is too slow but ignore its simplified characterization.

The most promising course will therefore be to compare a selection of critical standards and aesthetic formulae with necessary and hypothetical principles of conduct. But we must first distinguish a class of technical maxims which we have had no occasion to discuss so far.

9

TECHNICAL MAXIMS

A PAINTER should produce an effective artefact of paint on canvas, not reproduce an effective subject. A sculptor should make his work effective from whatever angle it is seen. A poet should prefer the concrete image to the abstract idea. A story-teller should refrain from an explicit moral. Writers of all kinds should avoid second-hand phrases, prefer the exact word to the euphonious one, use active rather than passive verbs. Jazz should be improvised, the film should address the eye rather than the ear, the making of a pot or a dress should accord with its function and exploit the distinctive qualities of the material chosen.

These are technical maxims for the artist, based on experience of what can and cannot be done with a particular medium. They are empirical discoveries, made as the possibilities of the medium are explored, used when they are helpful and discarded as soon as they prove a hindrance. Like other kinds of technical maxim, rule and instruction, they are justified by factual evidence that the means recommended is appropriate to the end in view. You prove the soundness of the instruction 'Press Button B' by getting your money back, or, if you refuse to be convinced that this is no accident, by taking the mechanism to pieces and confirming that pressure on the button does release the coins. The artist has no fixed instructions to follow, and cannot put much trust in the maxims which guide him, among other reasons because he is aiming at, or groping towards, a new effect, and precedents may fail him. However, he tests his maxims in the same way, by considering why the means is supposed to further the end, and looking for examples in which it does or does not.

A writer should avoid second-hand phrases—clichés if you prefer, but the pejorative name begs the question. Why? Because frequent repetition of a combination of words, or any other stimulus, weakens its effect: 'lily-white hand' has exhausted its power to evoke the colour. Yet many past traditions of poetry, you may object, used standard epithets which do not offend us as clichés; even 'lily-white hand' keeps its freshness in a Scots ballad. Poets have used them for other reasons besides laziness; we need to look more closely at their various functions. But is there not the difference that repetition kills more quickly in a time of mass media, since language degenerates faster and the constant task of renewing it is much harder? Perhaps; but the determination to avoid clichés at any cost also prevents writers saying what they are trying to say. We might consider, for example, why Robert Graves in his poem *Vanity* gets away with conventional imagery which many of his contemporaries would not risk, and so on indefinitely.

Such precepts have nothing to do either with subjective preference or with the objective value claimed for works of art. Presented with the maxim, 'The more scene and the less summary in a novel the better', no one is likely to answer that personally he likes as much summary as possible. No question of taste is involved; the claim is that a novel, however fine or degraded the taste to which it appeals, will achieve its effect more adequately if we see and hear the characters rather than merely hear about them. If you object that Lawrence's *Rainbow* succeeds in spite of ignoring this maxim, you need not insist on the value of what he was trying to do, only on his success in doing it. A compulsive thriller with more summary than scene would be just as striking an exception.

A creative artist, interested in his fellows largely for the sake of what he learns from them, tends to measure their importance by the technical principles useful to himself. His interest in predecessors who share his technical preoccupations, and his indifference to those who have nothing to teach him, are soon reflected in critical approval and disapproval. Confusion between technical maxims and critical standards becomes inevitable whenever the former win the status of dogmas. Even if it is clearly seen that obedience to them is at best a pre-condition of value, it is assumed that disobedience excludes the possibility of value. Thus it is still a valid discovery that observing the unities of space, time and action is a useful way to concentrate dramatic effect. But as soon as critics pronounced that the unities are not merely useful but necessary means to the tragic effect, they committed themselves to denying the value of any pretended tragedy which ignores them.

A very common variety of this fallacy is the presumption that an art was never any good before the discovery of some spectacular device, or ought never to have used some technique which has temporarily exhausted its possibilities. Technically an art progresses like a science, but after a certain point in its development cannot use all its resources at once, so that the presence or absence of one device has no bearing on the value of a work. But certain technical inventions give the illusion of discrediting everything which came before them. All painting without linear perspective seemed obsolete for some four hundred years after its discovery; Indian music is only just beginning to break down our preconception that to deserve attention music must have harmony as well as melody and rhythm; silent films became old-fashioned for all but film-society audiences within a couple of years of the first sound pictures. On the other hand nearly every movement in twentieth-century painting has denied itself some of its potential resources and evolved principles which make a virtue out of the sacrifice. Linear perspective is the very least of the devices to go overboard; Post-Impressionism disdained literary content in the interests of formal design; Surrealism scorned design and revived one limited kind of literary content; Abstract Expressionism moves away from both for the sake of exploring texture.

It is easy to find puritanical arguments in favour of the righteousness of such abstinence. Thus defenders of Post-Impressionism used to argue that painting, among other reasons because it is confined to a moment of time, cannot reproduce and interpret external reality as well as literature can; therefore we should purify it by taking away everything which it happens to share with literature. But do not the functions of different media overlap in any case? Painting can reproduce visual appearance better than writing can; it would be as plausible to argue that we should improve poetry by discarding visual imagery. Painting, being confined to two dimensions, cannot compete in formal construction with architecture; should it not attain complete purity by purging itself of architectural as well as literary elements? For all I know some theoretician of Abstract Expressionism may have used this argument seriously.

Technical maxims are guides for the artist, not standards for the critic. From the spectator's point of view, they explain why an artist succeeded or failed in making his effect, not whether he succeeded, let alone whether his effect is good or bad. It is an open question whether we who look at works of art instead of making them would not be better off if we had never heard of such rules. We are always in danger of refusing to enjoy a piece of sculpture because it is effective only from the front, a painting because we can or cannot recognize the subject, a poem because it uses conventional imagery, a film because the actors stand still and talk in front of a stationary camera. Unfortunately such false standards are much easier to apply than true ones. It is as though we were to point out unrecommended features in an athlete's technique as proof that he cannot have won the race, without bothering to find out whether he did or not.

NECESSARY STANDARDS

TECHNICAL maxims recommend means to an effect, critical standards value the effect. The purpose of this section is to clarify a number of standards variously named and interpreted by critics, and show that they are necessary according to the procedure laid down in part I, chapter 3.

I. UNITY WITHIN VARIETY

Of all the formulae which aestheticians have proposed as definitions of Beauty, the oldest, most persistent and, within its limits, most successful, is 'Unity within Variety'. It is a fact, which for the moment we shall examine without raising questions of value, that many works of art are so organized that the effect of any part depends on and contributes to the effect of the whole. Every art has developed means of articulating diverse responses—balance and proportion, melody, rhythm and harmony, metre and rhyme, the plot construction by which, according to Aristotle, the action is 'a complete whole, with its several incidents so closely connected that the transposal or withdrawal of any one of them will disjoin and dislocate the whole'. But these are only surface evidence of a structure in which one can continue analysis down to the brush-strokes under the microscope or the texture of meaning in a single line of verse without ever ceasing to discover new differences and new interrelations. The progressive mastery of the technique of integrating elements in a coherent whole is an important line of development in the history of art forms. In the visual arts, for example, Wölfflin's scheme, which fits several traditions fairly plausibly, distinguishes an 'archaic' stage in which the co-ordination of parts is still imperfect, a 'classical' stage in which the parts are fully integrated but remain distinct, and a 'baroque' stage in which the parts lose their separate identities in the whole. In the drama the ideal of structural unity goes back to the Greeks, in the novel it is as recent as the nineteenth century.

Formal integrity is as important in the arts of other cultures as in ours. We can be quite sure of this, in spite of the innumerable possibilities of misunderstanding unfamiliar styles; for although it is easy to overlook structural unity it is impossible to misunderstand it seriously or be mistaken in recognizing its presence. The little diagrams in textbooks of psychology which change before our eyes, from concave to convex and back again, are very simple; the more parts are interrelated, the less chance there is of relating them in more than one way. Admiring an African figure which I take for a demon, I am disconcerted to learn that it is a beneficent god; but if I find it satisfying as a shape, it does not worry me to learn that African sculptors never talk about the formal relationships which excite me. The interrelation of the parts, even if the sculptor feels only that he intensifies the magic potency by disposing them this way, cannot be accidental; although less easily analysed, it is as plainly objective as mere symmetry would be. This is especially obvious when listening to Oriental music, since the uninitiated Westerner cannot help trying to organize the notes in relation to his own musical system. Whenever he seems to recognize the beginning of a melody the next note is always wrong; the attempt to impose a false pattern is defeated as soon as it starts. After he has learned to rid himself of preconceptions and let the music take its own shape, he may still be alarmed to learn that his emotions are quite unlike those of the mode on which the musician is improvizing. But whatever else he may misunderstand, he cannot be mistaken about what he has perceived of the formal organization; he cannot hear melodies and rhythms which are not there. A great deal of our experience of the arts of remote cultures consists of the wrong reactions in the right interrelations.

A unified work of art is often compared to a living organism, in which the functioning of each member depends on the functioning of the whole. A common definition of the Unity within Variety, both in works of art and in organisms, is the one already quoted from Aristotle; no part can be altered without altering the effect of the whole. In both cases this needs qualification. A poet may feel that a single misprinted word has ruined the entire poem. Yet a very large proportion of the world's best art and literature survives as defaced pictures, broken statues and corrupt manuscripts, disfigured by restoration and interpolation, obscured by difficulties of language and symbolism. Granted that in each case damage has altered the effect of the whole to some degree, the more remarkable fact is that the total effect of a successful work, like the functioning of an organism, can stand a great deal of injury to its peripheral parts. One might even say that it heals; the context alters the significance of the misprinted word so that, with luck, it may seem to readers the right word. It is not so much that the alteration of any part affects the whole as that the significance of any part alters when it is detached from the whole.

For reasons considered in the introduction to this section, it will do us no good to suppose that Unity within Variety is the description of a quality called Beauty in the object we are contemplating. But in any case this object is merely a piece of canvas streaked with paint, a lump of chiselled stone, a series of sounds or marks on paper; it is a tool used by the artist to make us sense, imagine, think and feel in certain ways. Speaking of the balance of a picture does not imply that tampering with one side will make it turn over on the easel, and speaking of its unity implies, not that alteration of a line will make the rest shift on the canvas, but that it will modify our reactions to the rest. The question of the value of Unity within Variety may therefore be presented in this form: 'Is it simply a matter of subjective taste whether I prefer to imagine, think and feel in a wide variety of ways which harmonize with each other or in a small variety of ways which interfere with each other?'

As far as Unity is concerned, the answer is simple. Activities ought not to interfere with each other, and the more they assist each other the better; this is a standard already proposed as necessary.[1] Variety presents a more complicated problem. We may distinguish three classes of activities.

A. Activities directed to an end, for example a military campaign. Unity is necessary, but we generally prefer economy to variety. The campaign is well or ill organized by objective tests, independent of the value of its goal. Its manœuvres must be co-ordinated so that they assist each other, but the fewer there are the better.

B. Activities enjoyed for themselves, for example a holiday. Here we do favour variety, because doing one thing only is monotonous, and novelty helps to sustain interest. But this is a psychological generalization, not a necessary principle. If all you want to do on your holiday is fish, then a place where there is nothing to do but fish is as good as one where you can fish, swim and play tennis.

C. Activities with the end of enhancing the capacity to act, for example physical exercises. Here unity and variety are equally necessary. Co-ordination is not, as in the other classes, a means, but one of the ends; and the degree to which exercise enhances the general capacity for swift, effortless and spontaneous muscular co-ordination increases with the variety of movements exercised.

Whether Unity within Variety is a necessary standard depends therefore on the kind of response which a painting, building, poem or novel excites in us. Reading a novel simply for fun, aware that we shall forget it tomorrow without being appreciably altered for better or for worse, is an activity of type B. The novel's unity is only a means of concentrating an enjoyable effect, its variety only a means of keeping the reader's interest. But there are also novels which we read in the knowledge that their strong points, if we understand them, and their weaknesses, if we do not see through them, will influence the

[1] Cf. p. 33.

way we think, feel and act after we put the book down. We do not simply enjoy them; they enhance or reduce our capacity to enjoy. Among other effects, they influence our capacity to discriminate between objects and respond in accordance with their differences, without confusion, conflict or inhibition. A work of art heightens this capacity to the extent that our response to it is both various and unified; therefore within this class Unity within Variety is necessarily good.

The establishment of a class within which this standard is necessary also provides a criterion for distinguishing art from entertainment. Poems, paintings, music are art rather than entertainment to the extent that they have lasting effects, good or bad, on the way we sense, imagine, think and feel. But the distinction is not absolute; standards apply in varying degrees, and art is not a category to which a work does or does not belong. All art is more or less entertaining, all entertainment affects, in however minute a degree, the values of ordinary life.

Some of the most illuminating literary criticism consists of little more than pointing out interrelations and separating different strands of meaning, noting, for example, how a recurring image joins seemingly unrelated contexts yet itself changes significance as it changes context. Such criticism is not simply exposition; it is assumed, with no offer of proof except an implicit appeal to the test of the reader's own experience, that no one can wake to these connections and distinctions without thinking more highly of the work. This is not a groundless assumption. A critic exploring the structure of a work cannot show its degree of unity and variety, since these are not measurable quantities; but by pointing out crucial relations and differences he can, if we have not noticed them before, prove to us that it is more various and unified than we thought. (A critic can never prove the value of a work from scratch, but he can give us reasons for modifying our estimates in the direction of his own.) In doing this he also proves that it is better than we thought, by a standard which has nothing to do with private tastes.

How do we know whether reactions are successfully integrated or remain in conflict? Some critics tend to suppose

G

that complexity is always good, that if responses are simulta-
neous the writer has reconciled them, that there is no greater
compliment to a poem than to prove that it is a tangle of incompatible emotions. There is no reason to doubt that the
power to combine normally conflicting responses is one mark
of a good artist. Happy, we prefer not to remember death, and
a reminder of it depresses us; but a poet fuses the joy of life
and regret for its transience in a single mood. Feeling sorry
for an odd-looking man, we no longer think him funny, or
feel guilty if we do; but a good comedian is funny and pathetic
at once. In both cases some of the capacity to articulate outlasts the experience, and makes it insensibly easier to reconcile
the same contrasts in ordinary life. Yet a Cinemascope
devotional spectacle about Christians thrown to the lions also
arouses the most diverse reactions, sentimentality, lust, reli-
giosity, sadism, not only in different sequences but simulta-
neously. These reactions are surely muddled, not reconciled;
over-indulgence in them will reduce, not enhance the audience's
capacity to integrate experience. But how are we to show that
they are muddled?

Responses can be reconciled when their objects are different, cannot when their objects are the same. The pity and
cruelty excited by the martyrs in the film, and indeed in plenty
of more serious religious art, conflict in a way that the pity
and terror of tragedy do not. Pity and cruelty have the same
object, the pain of another, and one can grow only at the
other's expense. Pity makes us want to relieve the pain, cruelty
to increase it; the unstable compound can last only as long as
we refuse to recognize one of the components. On the other
hand pity for a wounded animal and fear of it have different
objects. Fear is likely to inhibit pity but is compatible with it,
since we pity the beast's suffering and are afraid of its claws,
and it may be possible to relieve the former without getting
in the way of the latter. The destructive process in the tragic
hero can work in us too; we pity him, fear it in ourselves. In
this case, unlike the case of the wounded animal, the objects
of pity and terror are interdependent, so that the two emotions
interact and lift each other to the highest pitch. Similarly, dis-

approval of crime is consistent with respect for a criminal's boldness and intelligence, but not with respect for him as a hero who does what we all would if we dared. The former combination in a novel may alter for the better the attitude of a reader who sees any reservation in condemning the man as an excuse for the crime. But the second attitude is profoundly contradictory; the disapproval makes the respect half-hearted, the respect degrades the moral condemnation to an inhibited man's envy or the fear of being a consistent rebel even in imagination.

2. SPONTANEITY

It is common to praise a work of art as effortless, natural, vital, spontaneous, or object to it as artificial, contrived, laboured, forced, wooden, lifeless. The simplest definition of 'spontaneous' action is action without thought, and the demand for spontaneity in the arts involves us at once in the question of the rôles and the relative merits of intelligence and unpremeditated impulse. For extreme enemies of intellectualism, only spontaneity matters; barren analysis kills the spirit, not to think is the precondition of creation and appreciation alike, and the sole test of value is the presence or absence of an inner vitality sensed by the intuition of the spectator. At first sight it may seem obvious that a taste for vitality or for intelligence is a matter of temperament and beyond argument. Yet even the most extreme rationalist, if he is interested in the arts at all, will hardly insist that it is possible to construct a good poem by analytic thought alone, or that to criticize a work as lifeless and contrived is never just.

Thinking helps us in some kinds of activity, in others is irrelevant, in others still is harmful. The question of thought and spontaneity in the arts covers a number of separate issues, and there is no reason to take the same side on all of them. In the first place, there is a sense in which a work of art undeniably has to be 'alive', and in which I do not have to think to discover whether it is alive. It must evoke some response, actively stimulate me to imagine, think and feel. A novel is lifeless in this sense if I cannot visualize the scenes it so meticulously describes, cannot get interested in the characters, remain emotionally inert through all their changes of fortune and misfortune. What I judge by standards is my response, and if the work excites no response, of course it is valueless for me. Further, I do not reason in order to discover whether I am responding. The question 'How do you know the work is alive?' is equivalent to 'How do you know it moves you?' and is as meaningless as any other demand for reasons to justify immediate experience. Many people have not learned to respond to poetry or music, and therefore have nothing to which they can apply aesthetic standards; in this sense it is a truism that it is useless to reason about art unless you can feel it.

A dead thing is inert, a living thing is responsive to stimulation, a person who 'radiates vitality' is more than usually responsive. A work is alive for me to the degree that I respond, which may have little relation to the experience of the artist; a masterpiece is dead for me when I am dead to it, and I may react violently, like a small boy watching a cowboy film, to a work put together listlessly by tired hacks. However, if I put no more nor less into the work than the artist did, then the artist himself was responsive, alive, vital. But this vitality is no more a distinguishing quality of the work of art than responsiveness is a distinguishing quality of my response. If we suggest any test of vitality to put beside the other critical standards, it immediately turns into one of the other standards. For example, we might say that vitality implies a fluid and sensitive response to the varying aspects of things, and a spontaneous mutual adjustment of interdependent activities. But this is Unity within Variety; the supreme example of a whole made up of mutually dependent parts is the living organism.

After several lifeless chapters, in which the writer thinks and feels in a perfectly conventional way, his personal vision and individual style suddenly emerge, and the book comes to life. Shall we conclude that vitality has something to do with a capacity to think and feel unconventionally? But the new feature which awakens the apathetic reader is individuality, the capacity to respond in accordance with one's own needs, not in conventional ways laid down by others with different needs. We now possess a new standard, but it has no more nor less to do with vitality than any of the others. Individuality (which by the present definition does not necessarily imply being unlike others) is good *a priori*. How far one man's needs differ from another's is an empirical question; but to the extent that they do it is a necessary principle that he ought to react differently from others, since his reactions are right or wrong in relation to ends of his own.

When someone declares that vitality, which you either do or do not feel, is more important than any of the qualities which critics discuss, he is not really talking about the qualities of a work of art, but prescribing how we ought to approach it. He is pronouncing that it is more important to feel than to analyse critically. What this means depends on which and how many of its meanings he is giving to 'feel'. If the word indicates the total response, then, as we have seen, it clearly is more important to feel than to analyse, since there is nothing to analyse unless the critic is already responding. One cannot measure value by standards without feeling anything, as one measures the length of a line with a ruler. Admittedly there have been critics who seemed to do this, rejecting tragedies which did not observe the three unities, and condemning an epic on the life of Joan of Arc because the career of a woman is unsuitable for epic treatment. A person completely insensitive to literature could pass such judgments on the basis of a hearsay account of the plot. But such labour-saving principles are technical maxims disguised as critical standards; it is impossible to apply genuine critical standards to a work without responding to it. For example, an art critic's observations about design, balance, proportion, weight, masses, volumes, are unintelligible to a spectator who responds to subject-matter but not to line and colour; he is very likely to take them as meaningless verbiage or deliberate mystification. Even when a critic does analyse to the point of dislocating his own response, he is not refusing to feel; he is hypersensitive to the parts but has forgotten how to put them together again. One cannot even misuse William Empson's procedures for exploring ambiguity without being extremely responsive to the resonance of isolated words and to their mutual repercussions when juxtaposed out of their context; the method goes wrong when the critic loses his sense of how the words are actually functioning within the poem.

There is another feeling which may be judged more important than critical analysis—not the response as a whole, but the feeling that the work is good. Unless we postulate a special aesthetic sense, we must conclude that to feel that a work is good is simply to enjoy it. We must therefore put the claim in another form: it is better to enjoy good art, and spontaneously prefer it to bad, than to evaluate critically without enjoying. In defence of this claim, let us consider another dispute between Messrs. A and B. A expresses a liking for a certain book, B raises objections. The book, according to B, encourages an unrealistic view of life; over-indulgence in escapist literature will weaken A's hold on facts, so that his enjoyment, like a taste for opium, will have harmful effects in the long run. His objection, then, is to A *liking* the book; reading and fully responding would be harmless if he spontaneously disliked it. If responding were beneficial or harmful in itself, a reader's level of sensibility would rise and fall in abrupt spurts with every book he read. But to enjoy or dislike a writer's way of looking at the world is to be disposed, among other things, to revert to it or react against it in the future. If B, in spite of his criticisms, reads the book himself with secret enjoyment, it is of no use to him to know in theory that it is bad; its effects are still harmful. On the other hand if he dislikes it spontaneously, the book would still be harmless even if he were unaware of his present reasons for pronouncing it bad. Clearly, too, B needs to be sure whether he enjoys the book or not; it would be dangerous to coax himself into believing that he cannot like it because he knows it is bad. It follows that critical judgments are not substitutes for spontaneous likes and dislikes, but means of checking them, educating them, and disputing over them. Presented with the choice between two extreme cases, a naturally, unconsciously sound taste is better than a joyless skill in critical analysis.

However, the argument is that it is better to enjoy *good* art than to criticize without enjoying. If someone boasts that he does not need to think because 'I can feel it, here', the soundness of his feeling is still a question for other people. Quite possibly it is sound; if he has a highly developed knack of discriminating between and co-ordinating impressions, a slight bristling of the hairs at the nape of his neck may be a better test for him than the analysis of distinctions and interrelations. But even if we were to admit his claim to a special intuition, the fact remains that he often disagrees with others who make the same claim, and there is no further intuition by which we perceive that his intuition is surer than theirs. We can argue with him only in relation to critical standards. However good his taste may be, without standards he has no means of educating it, no warning when it fails him in a particular case, no test of whether it is developing or degenerating, no basis for disputing with others.

'Vital' and 'alive' are the most general of such commendatory words as 'moving', 'exciting', 'interesting' and 'thrilling'. There is no need to give evidence when using them; it is enough that the work moved and excited the speaker, who invites his audience to try whether it moves and excites them too. 'Effortless', 'natural', 'spontaneous' are words which operate rather differently. When a man acts without thought or effort, we may either condemn him as thoughtless or applaud the spontaneity of the action, according to whether we believe that thought and effort are appropriate to the occasion. Unlike vitality, spontaneity therefore has tests which are independent of other critical standards; we need to be satisfied both of the absence and of the undesirability of deliberation and exertion in any particular case. Spontaneity is a favourite word of those who do not believe in critical tests; but it is noticeable that people who are content to trust their feelings, although invulnerable to artificiality and intellectual contrivance, are generally easy victims of forced, over-excited, over-insistent emotion. Is Henry Miller or John Osborne a writer who spontaneously expresses powerful emotions? Or does he use words to whip up emotion in himself, terrified of the apathy into which he would relapse if he let up even for a moment? If I am content to feel, and value the work by the strength of its kick, I cannot even ask the question.

Outside the arts, the value of spontaneity is an important question in the borderland between voluntary and involuntary activities. There are many kinds of activity in which we co-ordinate movements more swiftly and efficiently without thought than with it; thinking what to do next would kill the tightrope walker. The question arises in a different way in connection with emotion, which is 'genuine', 'sincere', only when it is spontaneous. We cannot decide to fall in or out of love, abolish a desire, repent a crime, experience a mystical illumination. We can, however, prepare by thought and effort the conditions in which the emotion may spontaneously come or go. The disappointed lover can try a change of scene, the tempted man can keep away from temptation, the sinner prays and is vouchsafed the gift of repentance, the mystic disciplines himself by contemplation and awaits the moment of insight. We can also find means of temporarily exciting the emotion, for example deliberately heeding only those aspects of the situation which evoke it. Such forced emotions are insincere and false, in the sense that they last only as long as the effort which sustains them, misleading the man who feels them and anyone else who, measuring their strength and duration by their apparent cause, uses them as signs for interpreting and anticipating his behaviour.

The response to a work of art includes both voluntary and involuntary activities. It may include thinking and even, through the characters in a novel, willing and deciding, as well as emotion. Whether we prefer its emotion to be spontaneous or forced is clearly not a matter of taste. There may be something to be said, on prudential grounds, for being the master of an artificially warm smile which deceives others and which is so automatic that I use it even when speaking on the telephone; but if it deceives me too, if I begin to forget the difference between the artificially warm feelings which it induces and my spontaneous affections, it has reduced my self-knowledge and my capacity for correct choice.

Bad artists are notoriously adept at hiding from us the always obscure dividing line between spontaneous and contrived feeling. The indistinct picture of the lost child or dying mother excites less pity than it would in any vague hearsay report of real people who do not concern me, but the over-emphatic words excite much more; the tears swell in my eyes, and I compliment myself on being more compassionate than I am. This objection to contrivance does not of course discredit rhetorical conventions which, like polite formulae in social intercourse, seem to exaggerate emotion but assume an understanding between author and reader as to the weight to be given to them.

But an activity cannot be spontaneous unless its co-ordination with willed activities is also spontaneous. Learning to swim, for example, or to ride a bicycle, involves both voluntary and involuntary adjustments. The learner follows instructions to perform collections of isolated voluntary actions; at a certain point, unpredictable for himself, all the voluntary and involuntary movements interact and order themselves spontaneously, and he finds himself staying afloat or keeping the bicycle upright. From this point even the actions which were formerly willed become spontaneous. Similarly, the individual style of speech and gesture which we call 'personality', a code of etiquette, the movements of an athlete, of a skilled craftsman and, arriving by easy stages at the arts, of an actor and of a dancer, involve a spontaneous co-ordination of both voluntary and involuntary movements. In all these cases we recognize spontaneity as a virtue, but the thinking to which we object is outside the system not within it. We are oppressed if someone's manners are too studied, if he is always thinking what to do and say next. But this does not mean that conversation, if it is to be polite, must never be intelligent; intelligence is a virtue within the frame of manners, and has nothing do to with the value of effortless politeness undistracted by questions about the polite thing to do. In the same way, the organization of a work of art, since it involves both voluntary and involuntary activities, should be spontaneous; but this has nothing to do with the value of intelligence inside the work, which is valuable to the same degree and for the same reasons as in ordinary life. For example, in Thomas Mann's *Magic Mountain* the thinking of Settembrini and Naphta is at the very centre of the book, but there are also places where cracks open in the structure and we glimpse Mann himself thinking. In the *Hysterica Passio* chapter the tension and nervous outbreaks in the hospital seem contrived because, although the preceding events do not explain them, we can see why the author put them in; the hospital is a microcosm of the sick world, and it is nearly 1914.

It is notorious that months and years of effort may be needed to produce an effortless poem, and only a single rapturous burst of inspiration to produce a laboured one. Spontaneity has nothing to do with the method or creation; it implies only that the thought and effort of the creative process leave no traces in the completed work. Artists hide the traces of their labour with varying success, so that we can credit their work with spontaneity only in varying degrees. It would be absurd to reject Eliot's poetry as laboured and contrived, but reading it after Yeats' one cannot quite forget what hard work it must have been to write it. But the critical standard that the effect of the completed work should be spontaneous is easily confused with the very questionable technical maxim that thought and effort should be avoided in the process of creation. It may be admitted in favour of this maxim that if we look for examples of pure spontaneity, in which the intrusive will and intellect of the artist are reduced to absolute zero, the most convincing claimants are works which are indeed the achievement of a single undistracted creative act—improvized music, Chinese ink painting, *Kubla Khan* if you take Coleridge's word that he wrote it in an opium dream. There is a unique satisfaction in this kind of expression, which, if one is in the mood for it, makes the whole of written music and the whole of Western painting seem artificial; but we cannot, unless we are willing to rank Louis Armstrong above Bach, admit that it is the best of art except in this single respect. In any case pure mindless creation is not a practical possibility for anyone working on a larger scale or with less tractable material; there is no alternative to compromise between conscious effort and spontaneous imagination.

It is often supposed that there is a contradiction between the rival claims of order (Unity within Variety) and spontaneity in the arts. Classicists, it is assumed, value art for its order, which can be imposed only by reason; romantics prefer spontaneity and do not mind disorder. On the one hand there is Racine, coolly and intelligently constructing flawless tragedies, on the other Shakespeare, whose untrammelled genius bursts the confines of rational order. But this dichotomy involves confusion between technical and critical questions. It is clearly a fact that creative imagination without rational control often fails to achieve coherent organization, and also a fact that too much thought may leave an effect of contrivance; discovering a practical compromise between these extremes is a technical problem for artists, who are not bound to solve it always in the same way. Whether Racine or Shakespeare inclined to one or the other method of writing is a rather unprofitable historical question, depending for its solution on biographical information and on such evidence as psychologists can extract from the completed works. But from the point of view of criticism the best tragedies of Shakespeare and Racine alike are both orderly and spontaneous. The assumption that *Lear* is formless in comparison with *Phèdre* was plausible only when there were no tests of structural integration below the level of plot construction. Modern literary criticism has discovered new methods of exploring structure, for example the analysis of interrelated images; we now understand that *Lear* too is an intricately organized play within which the effect of any part is inseparable from the whole. On the other hand, in Racine's play, as in Shakespeare's, the effects of the parts *do* interact and influence each other; he has not simply laid them side by side in an artificial order, inferring from literary precedents that they *ought* to interact. We respond to them in their interrelations, and do not, as in the example from the *Magic Mountain* mentioned above, have to reconstruct the reasons which led the author to put them in this order. *Phèdre* is spontaneous in the only sense that matters; we never catch sight of the author thinking what to write next. Both poets successfully avoid the dangers both of uncontrolled imagination and of intellectual construction, disorder in the one case and contrivance in the other. We might say that the test of success in 'classicist' art is whether it is spontaneous, in 'romantic' whether it is orderly.

The only meaning of 'spontaneity' which provides a separate critical standard is negative, the absence of thought and effort. When we think of spontaneity as positive, we are using the word as synonymous with 'vitality'; but, as we have seen, every quality approved by critical standards contributes to vitality, including order itself. The play, whether Shakespeare's or Racine's, is a system of interdependent parts like a living organism, and its power to move us is the reinforcement of the effect of each part by the effect of the rest. The force of a blow depends on co-ordination of the muscles of the arm. Think how to articulate muscular movements, and you cannot lift your arm; but it is no advantage to have muscles which move spontaneously without co-ordination. The twitchings of a paralytic are as spontaneous as the motions of an athlete.

3. TRUTH

'Truth' is the word by which we express almost any kind of approval of any kind of utterance. Critics and aestheticians have always been fond of it, most of all when they have least to say. Defenders of the arts against their great rivals the sciences especially favour the word, as well as its companion 'Reality'; scientific information is true, poetry is even truer. Although it is convenient to discuss the claim that 'Beauty is truth' under the heading *Necessary standards*, it confuses principles of all three kinds, technical, hypothetical and necessary. Here it will be enough to distinguish eight, several of which appear in other chapters under other names.

(i) *Truth to material* (technical)

An artist should exploit the distinctive properties of his material, avoiding effects for which it is unsuited. Sculptors should not carve wood as though they were carving marble.

(ii) *Sensuous accuracy* (technical)

A writer should reproduce the exact curve of what he sees, selecting the typical yet distinguishing detail. Critics seldom use the word 'truth' in this connection, but for some aestheticians this is the whole secret of the artist's penetration to the underlying Reality. Sensuousness is necessarily good, catching the exact curve is an important but dispensable means to it.[1]

(iii) *Consistency with utilized fact or legend* (technical)

A writer, whenever his effect depends on the reader's knowledge of external facts and legends, should get them right. If he writes 'I took the Northern Line to Piccadilly', the names contribute nothing to the illusion if the reader does not know the London Underground system, spoil it if he does. It would not be a positive literary merit if the writer had avoided the mistake; he has a perfect right to invent an imaginary underground system; but since he has chosen to clarify his route by calling on our knowledge of an existing system, he should respect our knowledge. He can invent a convention by which English and Americans speak the same stylized language, but if he tries to reproduce the actual differences very slight infidelities in rhythm and vocabulary will destroy the illusion. However far the writer's imaginary world diverges from the one we know, he cannot quite escape this duty, since he must build it from components known to us, the basic units of which are words with known meanings. Simply by writing the name 'Rome', a poet appeals to factual and legendary information of the reader's—that Rome used to be the seat of an Emperor and is now the seat of the Pope, for example. Factual truth of course is irrelevant; a mistake over the Northern Line is of the same order as an error in Greek mythology.

[1] Cf. chapter 10, section 4.

(iv) *Documentary authenticity* (hypothetical)

If a writer seeks to enlarge understanding of a particular situation, the situation in his story should resemble it on all points which affect understanding. Anything he teaches us about the manner of thinking and behaving of his diplomats, television stars, nuns or Teddy-boys will help us only to the extent that they resemble their prototypes outside the story. The way in which the novel and drama illuminate particular human types and situations, without necessarily adding to our stock of information, will be considered under *Hypothetical judgments*.[1] This illumination is not, of course, confined to social and political problems. To take an example from the preceding section, a novelist's reproduction of American and English speech may not stop at the level of accuracy necessary to sustain his illusion; it may enhance the reader's awareness of differences in rhythm and vocabulary which reflect differences between the American and English styles of life. But if his book is to survive into an age when the two dialects will no longer be distinguishable, of course it must have other merits. The value of documentary authenticity is hypothetical, depending on the situation and interests of the audience.

(v) *Truth to life* (necessary)

Characters in a story should behave as similar characters in life would behave in similar situations. Among the many senses in which a work of art may be called true, this is the only one which is at all like the scientific sense of truth, and at the same time recognized as important even by critics who would ignore documentary authenticity. It is the one place where the division between science and art presents a problem.

Many critics insist that no comparison with external fact can be relevant to judgment of a work of art, and no factual information can contribute to its value—that is, in our terminology, to its necessary value. Those who take this attitude are not escapists wishing to take refuge from life in art; they are simply aware of what can and cannot be done with different

[1] Cf. p. 139–145.

media. If an author wishes to convince us of a fact he has discovered about human behaviour, he should write a psychological or sociological treatise, giving us accurate case-histories,
tables of statistics and a full bibliography. If instead he writes
a fictitious quintessential case-history, he shirks the duty of
giving his evidence. Moreover, in order to make his story convincing, he has to hide from us the line where fact ends and
fiction begins. Readers may well dig interesting information
out of the story, but they will have to check it for themselves;
they cannot take the author's word for it. Indeed, the author
has not given his word; it is the reader who guesses that just at
this point in the story the author is writing directly from
experience. . . . And yet, in spite of all this, it is a plain fact that
novels and plays are among the more important sources of our
knowledge of human behaviour.

Here we must return to the distinction between objective
and subjective understanding discussed earlier.[1] Unquestion-
ably the novel is a bad medium for conveying objective knowledge about human behaviour, but it is a very good one for
teaching me to put myself in the place of others. The writer
makes me imagine a concrete situation and see it from the
points of view of characters perhaps very unlike myself. At the
moments when I think 'He wouldn't have done that' or 'Yes,
that's just what he would do', I am not depending on my
experience of similar characters outside the story; this 'he' is
'I with his character in his situation'. I cannot verify, by any
so far known external check, how a man would behave when
meeting his father's ghost, landing on Mars or living among
Lilliputians; yet I may feel quite confident that he would
not act as the author supposes, or that, although it never
occurred to me before, this is indeed exactly how he would
behave.

We judge by truth to life only to the extent that a character
is revealed subjectively. For example, a novel of Kafka im-
prisons me in the mind of the hero, K; however precisely it
records the external appearance and conduct of others, I
experience only K's illusory and frustrating glimpses inside

[1] Part 3, chapter 5.

them. I do not expect their behaviour to be true to life; I find it, not objectively improbable, but subjectively unintelligible, and share K's struggle to understand it. On the other hand, the novel would collapse if K himself were not utterly, prosaically true to life, if he did not behave exactly as I, if I were like him, would behave in his unintelligible situation.

The influence of psychological theories on novelists is instructive in this connection. If a novelist, in order to explain his hero's avarice in later life, were to present him in childhood playing with his own dung, we should not enjoy the shock of recognition that this is true to life. It is simply a bit of misplaced science, which explains nothing subjectively, although as an objective explanation it may be useful to psychologists. In Thomas Mann's *Magic Mountain*, Naphta challenges Settembrini to a duel. Settembrini meets him, but fires in the air. Naphta, unable to make him fight, raises his weapon and shoots—himself. The Freudian principle that frustrated aggression may turn back on the aggressor was no doubt in Mann's mind; it may also dispose us to accept the incident more readily than an earlier generation of readers might have done. But it is true for me only if I feel subjectively that Naphta, whose destructiveness pervades every aspect of his life and beliefs, would actually at this moment, his need to kill abruptly thwarted on the verge of fulfilment, rather kill himself than have no one to kill at all.

A novel makes me understand how a man like X would behave in a situation like Y. To the extent that people and situations in my own experience resemble X and Y, the novel helps me to understand them; but the degree to which it gives me such practical help is an accident of my personal history, and its usefulness to me is the hypothetical value of its documentary authenticity, discussed in the preceding section. When this is discounted, what remains? The novel, by placing me subjectively in new situations, has increased my capacity for subjectively understanding myself and others. This is necessarily good, since it increases my capacity for discovering facts relevant to the soundness of my decisions, which is necessarily good according to the opening argument of part I, chapter 3.

(vi) *Genuineness of feeling* (necessary)

Feeling should not be willed, forced, contrived. Cf. chapter 10, section 2, *Spontaneity*.

(vii) *Realistic view of life* (necessary)

The attitude to life reflected in a work of art should be consistent with external facts. The extent to which I resist the ineradicable tendency to mistake what I should like to happen for what will happen depends very much on the art on which I nourish my imagination. My resistance is weakened by uncritical surrender to a work which encourages me to think that the righteous will be rewarded and the wicked punished in this world, or that a little good will can solve basic conflicts, or that the worst men will prove when I get to know them to have hearts of gold, or that I can escape the consequences of my actions by a facile change of heart. An artist should enhance, not reduce, the capacity to 'face facts'.[1]

The extent to which such inconsistencies with fact mislead varies with the conventions in which the artist works. Stereotypes in place of characters, and their simple classification as black or white, are acceptable in a stylized convention, but in a professedly naturalistic story tempt us to imagine that people are more uniform and predictable than they are in fact. In a comedy we admire the ingenuity with which the author manipulates the plot so that everything turns out for the best; in a naturalistic convention, a story which leads logically to disaster yet ends happily weakens one's hold on facts.

An artist fosters an unrealistic view of life by obscuring either my vision of the external world or my own self-knowledge. To take an example of the latter, why is it that, as a picture of a man dying in the knowledge that he has wasted his life, Hemingway's brilliant story *The Snows of Kilimanjaro* seems false by the side of Tolstoy's *Death of Ivan Ilyitch*? Answering in general terms, it must be very unpleasant to die in this way, and in Tolstoy's story so it is; yet while reading Hemingway's story I find it rather agreeable to imagine myself

[1] See part I, chapter 3.

H

as a strong man who has experienced everything, passing with clear eyes through the last experience of all, complacently dis-illusioned, bullying a devoted woman who refuses to see the truth as nakedly as I do. My vanity, which always has a last trick up its sleeve, consoles me with the picture of myself as a man who needs no consolation. Nor is it misreading the story to identify myself with the hero in this way. In the *Death of Ivan Ilyitch* Tolstoy and I enter into the last months of the dying man with lucidity and compassion; in the *Snows of Kilimanjaro* Hemingway and I conspire to pretend that we are being ruthless with ourselves.

'The one experience that he had never had he was not going to spoil now. He probably would. You spoiled every-thing. But perhaps he wouldn't.'

The hero is about to pretend that he will not make a mess of his death, but sees through the pretence at once—a sequence which recurs several times in the story. Yet this honesty diverts attention from the claim that he has experienced everything. By his own account he has spent his life repeating about four experiences, women, sport, fighting, drinking, in one country after another, but he is dramatizing himself as a man who has drained the cup of life to the very lees. Also, there is the curious switch from the personal 'he' to the impersonal 'you' and back again. It is *you*, people in general, who spoil every-thing; it is *he* who is honest enough to know that he spoils everything and in the present case perhaps will not. This might be reading too much into the pronouns if it were not that throughout there is the same tendency to escape personal res-ponsibility by generalizing the weaknesses which he freely admits, changing himself into 'you' ('How could a woman know that you meant nothing that you said?'), his own life into 'it', life in general ('So this was the way it ended, in a bickering over a drink'). On both points the hero is reported without irony; the author does not see through his pose.

Is it possible to accept this description of what Hemingway is doing, yet answer 'It is all a question of taste; personally I

like stories which make life and death seem more comfortable
than they are'? Whatever is to my taste, I weaken my chances of
getting it by refusing to see things as they are.

(viii) *Metaphysical truth* (necessary)

The view of life reflected in a work of art should be a good one
to live by. This is not, of course, quite what metaphysicians
mean by 'metaphysical truth'; it is an interpretation, going
back to I. A. Richards' *Principles of Literary Criticism*,
which will occupy us at greater length in the last part of this
book.

A man's beliefs consist of:

A. His religious or philosophical ideas (true, false or
meaningless).

B. His 'attitude to life' or 'view of life' (good or bad), a
disposition to think, feel and act in one way rather than
another.

We tend to identify beliefs with ideas alone, and to treat
attitudes as their corollary. But a pessimistic view of life is a
tendency, other things being equal, to despair rather than to
hope; the pessimist does not necessarily accept as meaningful
and true such propositions as 'Everything is for the worst in
the worst of all possible worlds'. In the arts it is especially hard
to maintain the primacy of the idea. Music, and literature too
very often, communicate nothing but a capacity to feel and act
in certain ways; the ideas which music breeds in some listeners'
minds are probably very unlike the composer's, if he had any.
Beethoven's last works, like Shakespeare's, resolve his earlier
conflicts in a mood of serenity and reconciliation. A listener to
the last Quartets is tempted to look for words to define the
profound Truth which Beethoven grasped at the end of his
life; but Shakespeare, who did use words, philosophizes in his
final comedies only in brief passages which misrepresent him
as soon as we detach them from their context. These works
intimately change us, yet the ideas they seem to convey slip

through our fingers. Even when a writer's ideas are clear, we have no guarantee that he believes them intellectually or that emotionally they can mean to us what they mean to him. Baudelaire seems to have been intellectually a sceptic, yet perfectly convinced of the validity of a religious view of life (cf. his observation in *Fusées*: '*Dieu est le seul être qui, pour régner, n'ait même pas besoin d'exister.*'). The churches, Madonnas and Crucifixions of medieval other-worldliness and Renaissance humanism reflect the same ideas but utterly different attitudes to life.

Metaphysical propositions in a work of art have the same status as other kinds of disputable information. We suspend disbelief only for the time being; the artist cannot convince us of their truth, because art is a bad medium for proving anything. They can function only as pointers to a view of life, which we experience from the angle of the seer, explore emotionally and value for ourselves. We judge the view of life by the standards which we apply to the work as a whole, for example by the range of human experience it embraces or excludes, integrates or leaves in conflict, its 'realism' (cf. the preceding section), whether it is morally sound or unsound, affirmative or negative. Very different works of art, philosophies of life, codes of conduct, may be equally good by these standards; the contradictions between the philosophies of great artists need not trouble us.

A work is necessarily the better for a 'true' philosophy of life, which will help me, even if I do not accept it, to find my own way to live successfully. A work is also hypothetically better for a philosophy which is 'true for me', which directly answers my personal needs. The manner in which an artist can convert us to his own view of life may be illustrated by this passage from Gautier's *Mademoiselle de Maupin*, which struck many nineteenth-century readers with the force of a new Gospel:

'Je suis un homme des temps homériques;—le monde où je vis n'est pas le mien, et je ne comprends rien à la société qui m'entoure. Le Christ n'est pas venu pour moi; je suis aussi païen qu'Alcibiade et Phidias.—Je n'ai jamais été cueillir sur le Golgotha les fleurs de la passion, et le fleuve profond qui coule du flanc du crucifié et fait une ceinture rouge au monde, ne m'a pas baigné de ses flots:—mon corps rebelle ne veut point reconnaître la suprématie de l'âme, et ma chair n'entend point qu'on la mortifie.—Je trouve la terre aussi belle que le ciel, et je pense que la correction de la forme est la vertu. La spiritualité n'est pas mon fait, j'aime mieux une statue qu'un fantôme, et le plein midi que le crépuscule. . . .'

Here Gautier expresses no ideas whatever; he simply states his own attitude without disguise: '*Je suis* . . . *je trouve* . . . *j'aime*.' But George Moore, for example, wrote in his *Confessions of a Young Man*: 'Here was a new *creed* proclaiming the divinity of the body; and for a long time the reconstruction of all my *theories* of life on a purely pagan basis occupied my attention' (my italics). It would be a mistake to criticize this kind of conversion as merely emotional; so is any conversion from one view of life to another, however much auxiliary reasoning may contribute to it.[1] The only question is whether, in the context of one man's needs, the change is for the better, whether it releases suppressed wants, reconciles conflicting ones, permits acknowledgment of previously unwelcome facts. In Moore's case the change is from Shelleyan idealism to a view of life which is, one might argue, more consistent with his own self-knowledge; he no longer forces an unspontaneous idealism and interest in abstract ideas, and liberates an appetite for the concrete, sensuous and sensual of which he was formerly half ashamed.

We have considered 'reality' only as an adjunct of 'truth' in its various meanings; but there is one sense of 'real' which deserves separate examination. 'It was only then that the danger became real to me'—I had long recognized the danger in the abstract, but only then began to be afraid and make plans to avert it. Knowing that a thing exists, it remains unreal to me as long as I am numb to it, continue to act as though it did not exist. We do not use 'true' in quite this way, although we

[1] Cf. p. 170 f.

do use 'exist': 'Other people don't exist for him.' A successful work of art is intensely real in this sense, and tempts us to suppose that anything inside it which is absent from this world must be present in some other world, as an ideal form subsisting in a Platonic firmament, or, a modern and scientific-sounding version of the doctrine, as an archetype in the collective unconscious. Yeats, judging by his known beliefs, meant us to take him quite literally when in his *Second Coming* he wrote of glimpsing a 'vast image out of *Spiritus Mundi*':

> Somewhere in sands of the desert
> A shape with lion body and the head of a man,
> A gaze blank and pitiless as the sun,
> Is moving its slow thighs, while all about it
> Reel shadows of the indignant desert birds.

Certainly Yeats has made his Sphinx real for us. We see it rising from its hind legs, its forelegs not yet moving; we recognize how 'indignant' exactly fits the squawking and flapping of birds, and 'reel' the movement, not of the birds, but of their shadows on the sand; but this sensory exactness contributes only a little to the effect. Like some other mythical beasts in literature, Blake's tiger, Melville's white whale and the horse in Lawrence's *St. Mawr*, Yeats' Sphinx haunts us with the sense of a significance which cannot be wholly explained as the resonance of disturbed subconscious desires and terrors—an explanation which might satisfy us in the case of the monkey in Le Fanu's *Green Tea*, for example.

In this case it is fairly easy to disintegrate part of the poetic significance into a series of prose statements. Yeats writes explicitly in the opening stanza of the breakdown of civilized order in the nineteenth century; and the resurgent Sphinx concentrates in a single image multiple aspects of the rising barbarism and of Yeats' attitude to it. We forget that civilization is precarious, that barbarism sleeps but never dies (birds perching on the sleeping Sphinx). The new savagery is a revival of the subhuman within man, uniting human intelligence with bestial appetites (human head and lion's body). It is the denial of life (stone), sterile (desert), defiance of reason and order (the unnatural union of man, beast and lifeless stone). It is also the renewal of a mystery which is more than rational and more than human (the enigma and wisdom of the Sphinx, the animal gods of Egypt, the mindless gaze pitiless 'as the sun'). It is invincible, and its disruption of order is itself part of an ultimate order; the coming of this Antichrist is itself the Second Coming:

> And what rough beast, its hour come round at last,
> Slouches towards Bethlehem to be born?

Some of these implications are factual and even true. But any insistence that the value of the symbol depends on the truth of these prose implications would upset the poem's delicate balance on the edge of belief. Yeats presents disturbing possibilities condensed in an image which appears, 'troubles my sight', and vanishes. If the image is actually there in *Spiritus Mundi*, if savagery is invincible and even has the ultimate right on its side, are we to give up all hope for Western civilization? If it is not, was the whole poem a mistake?

4. SENSUOUSNESS

What is the difference between the prose statement 'The clock has struck twelve' and Shakespeare's 'The iron tongue of midnight hath told twelve'?

A general answer would be that the first tells us *that* the clock has struck twelve, the second makes us hear the strokes, touch the iron, see the tongue inside the bell, feel the irrevocable passage of time. Proceeding to details, the relatively strong stresses on the last five syllables, slowing down the movement of the line, suggests the intervals seeming to widen as one listens for the next stroke. The alliteration of T-sounds, three of which mark off the last four syllables sharply from each other, suggests the isolation of each successive stroke. The juxtaposition of 'iron' and 'tongue' intensifies by contrast one's sense of the unfeeling hardness of iron and the living softness of tongue. The word 'told' has two sets of associations, both reinforcing the preceding 'iron tongue'; it implies speech, counting, and links with 'tongue'; it also suggests 'tolled', linking with 'iron'. We listen with two opposing kinds of awe— for the inhuman strength of metal and the more than human solemnity of personified Midnight. Midnight 'tolls' the funeral of the day, and 'tells', counts off, the strokes of the hour, indifferent as unfeeling metal to human regret at the passage of time. There is no space to consider how many of the associations of 'midnight', as end, as beginning, as climax of literal and metaphorical darkness, are relevant to this line. It is enough that, even detached from its context in *A Midsummer Night's Dream*, the line has an intricate structure, only partly accessible to analysis with the present tools of literary criticism, and that within this structure rhythm, alliteration and syntax all serve to intensify, vary and articulate the sensuous and emotional implications of the words.

Analysing the line in this way, it seems to me that I am doing more than explaining certain differences between poetry and factual description, I am showing that it is good as poetry. Literary critics tend to work on the same assumption, pointing out imagery which is sensuously precise and vivid and emotionally evocative as though it were evidence that the poem is good. But why do we assume it? A common answer is that poetry restores the capacity to see with a child's eye, renews the sensuous and emotional aura which objects lose as we learn to treat them as tools for practical ends. The adult, to the extent that science and commerce have degraded his vision, fits things into categories determined by their conventional uses, forgets what they look and feel like, recognizes them by their labels and knows what they are for. Playing idly with a match-box he may suddenly recall what it meant for him as a child, when it was not only a receptacle, to keep a ladybird, perhaps, not matches, but an object to be enjoyed for its sharp rectangular shape, coloured label, sulphurous smell (now dimmed by over-smoking), the thinness and elasticity of the wood, and the feel

of its texture against the finger-tips. Yet one can hardly take it
for granted that the change from child to man is entirely
retrogressive. What is wrong with treating a match-box as a
thing to keep matches in? Is it necessarily a good thing that
poetry makes us be again as little children?

People who see no way of defending poetry against science
except by the claim that it tells a different and superior kind
of truth will say that the poet enjoys a disinterested vision of
things as they really are, while the scientist's concepts are
merely tools to manipulate them. Shakespeare's line describes
truly the concrete reality of the event; 'The clock has struck
twelve' makes an abstraction, useful if you want to know
whether it is time for bed. The most distinguished explorer of
this approach is Bergson, one of the few philosophers whose
aesthetic theory is genuinely illuminating even for those who
reject its metaphysical foundations; through T. E. Hulme's
Speculations it has influenced the practice of modern English
poetry. But a poet does not describe things, either truly or
falsely; he either succeeds or fails in making us see and otherwise sense them in imagination. However much critics misuse
the word 'truth', they praise the clarity, vividness, particularity,
not the truth of a poet's images. Admittedly the poet looks
for a metaphor which will, in Hulme's phrase, catch the 'exact
curve' of what he sees, and it is tempting to suppose that the
value of the metaphor lies in the exactness of this correspondence. But if this were so, metaphors would not wear out
and become clichés any more than factual statements do.
'Raven locks', 'cherry lips', 'satin skin', 'swan neck' are all
exact; the first, for example, catches admirably the glint of
blue in some black hair and in a raven's wing. We are not
impressed by the correspondence because these clichés no
longer serve their purpose, which is, not to describe the girl's
beauty, but to make us see it. Again, a poetic image does not
tell us something new which we verify by observation; it
works only if we have made the observation already. It makes
us imagine distinctly what we have already sensed vaguely.
'The violet hour' in Eliot's *Waste Land* means nothing unless
you have already seen the violet sky above the houses as you

go home from work; if you have never noticed any shade in the
sky between blue and black, the phrase is not even explicit
enough to show you what to look for.

The reader makes the picture, not the poet; and even the
coinciding detail which gives the shock of recognition is far
from indispensable. One is often surprised to notice how little
the poet has told us about visual appearance, how much we
have supplied for ourselves. There is absolutely no information
about the appearance of swallows and daffodils in these lines
from *A Winter's Tale*:

> Daffodils
> That come before the swallow dares, and take
> The winds of March with beauty.

What we know gets in the way of what we see; often a poet
deliberately defies our abstract knowledge in order to shock us
into actively imagining. However little we may respect the mere
abstractions of science, in what sense can we claim that the
poet's language is truer, closer to the concrete reality? It is no
reproach to him to say that his language would be false as
description, for he is not describing; he is exciting us to see,
and conventional descriptions are excuses for not seeing. Eliot
writes in his early *Morning at the Window*:

> The brown waves of fog toss up to me
> Twisted faces from the bottom of the street.

In what sense can it be truer to say that the fog is throwing up
faces than that the poet is looking down at faces through fog
blown by gusts of wind? This may seem like labouring the
point; but what is there in the poem which can be true or false?
A description of the scene can be true or false; so can a description of how the poet sees it, 'I look down through waves of
brown fog, blown by gusts of wind, at faces at the bottom of
the street distorted by the fog and by my angle of vision'; so
can the statement 'The poet's impressions are like mine when

I look down at faces through fog'; but the poet and the reader see, they do not refer.

Further, can it be seriously maintained that Eliot's purpose is to evoke a disinterested vision of the street as it really is? Certainly his vision is disinterested in the sense that he detaches things from their uses; the practical dangers of believing that faces can part from their owners and float in the fog do not hinder him. But he looks at things in this way in order to revive the emotional associations which weaken when we learn to treat things solely as means. Here they become agencies in the dreary disgust which informs the whole poem. The 'brown waves of fog' are a dirty sea; the faces are flotsam 'tossed up' contemptuously, one degree fouler than the city fog as flotsam is fouler than the sea; they are 'twisted' because they belong to twisted people, with, to quote other lines of the poem, 'damp souls' and 'aimless smiles'.

The plain fact that most poetic imagery is emotive is an obvious difficulty in the theory that its function is to reproduce reality. A poet's concern with visual detail and his refusal to mention his emotions do not imply that his imagery is not emotive; he knows that only the simplest emotions are describable,[1] and that the way to define an emotion is to define the object which excites it. Hulme laid the main stress on the exact reproduction of what the poet sees, but also exacted the secondary duty of reporting exactly what he feels. This might be plausible if poets carefully separated the object from their feelings, instead of fusing them indissolubly as they do in practice. How can we claim that the poet presents the object as it really is, when he manifestly projects his own emotions on to it, emotions which, if he has an individual talent, will be different from those which the same object excites in any other poet? Again, why are poets so little concerned about the way in which we visualize, so long as we respond with the right attitudes and emotions? As we have seen, they seldom fill in a picture, and the visualizations of any two readers no doubt differ as widely as the imaginations of two illustrators to a

---

[1] Cf. part 3, chapter 5.

novel; but this does not imply any basic disagreement in their understanding of the poem.

Rejecting the explanation of Bergson and Hulme, have we the right to decide as we please whether we prefer imagery to be distinct or blurred, emotionally neutral or rich and various? The important part of their thesis rests on foundations much firmer than metaphysical assertions about Reality and things as they truly are. The primary reason for doing or not doing something is that we like or dislike it. It is also necessary to do things which are neutral, but only as means to ends, of ourselves and others, which are enjoyable in themselves. It is therefore a necessary principle that the fewer activities we enjoy for themselves, the less successfully we are living. Other things being equal, it is better to enjoy one's job then to live only after working hours, better to marry for love than for money, better to take pleasure in helping people than to help them out of duty, better to buy a kitchen knife which pleases the eye and touch as well as doing its work than to buy it for its cutting edge alone. The diminution of sensuous and emotional responsiveness reduces the range within which we enjoy and suffer. Whenever we lose the capacity to sense an object and feel its attraction or repulsion, we reduce our reasons for living by one, saw a little deeper into the bough which supports us. We gain more means to fewer ends, and life has less and less 'meaning'—that is, there is less and less reason for acting one way rather than another, although routine keeps us working for ends which are themselves means to further ends which recede further and further into the distance.

The arts help to develop responsiveness, and without their counter-influence practical concerns and the analytic habit of mind tend to reduce it. But the conflict is not between a right and a wrong picture of the world. We need to be able to respond fully to a thing at one moment, and at another strip it of all emotional associations in order to study it analytically. The problem is to distinguish and co-ordinate two ways of dealing with an object, not to choose between two contradictory accounts of what the object really is. A good poem restores us to a world charged with meaning, in which things, detached from their uses, are again pleasing or displeasing in themselves. It is not a matter of subjective taste whether we prefer a poet to heighten sensitivity by a fresh image or dull it by a cliché.

5. AFFIRMATION

A work of art, it is often claimed, should be affirmative, positive, on the side of Life. Many excellent judges of the arts dispute this principle and scoff at any suggestion that we should value a work by the degree of hope it allows us. Is this an issue on which we must agree to differ?

Both sides in the dispute, although at different levels of taste, often share a common confusion between objective fact and subjective attitude. Middlebrow readers seeking comfort in a good book expect it to ignore all disagreeable facts. When there are so many nice things in the world, why must the author insist on writing about the nasty things? On the other side we find people talking as though a despairing vision of life may be objectively true, as though an artist does not hate or lose hope or despise, but discovers that life is objectively hateful, hopeless or despicable.

A reader who expects nothing from a novel except a little escapist pleasure has the right to be annoyed with a novelist who insists on reminding him of facts he wants temporarily to forget. But if a novel is to affect him permanently, increase his capacity for happiness instead of making him momentarily happy, the novelist's affirmation must be invulnerable to any fact which the reader may encounter after he throws the book away. On the other hand, granted that a writer can and must look directly at the facts to which it is hardest to reconcile ourselves, there remains the question whether a pessimist's vision of the world is the cause or the effect of his pessimism. In spite of Freud it is still common to assume that we should all be optimists if reality did not keep breaking in, that distorting spectacles are always rose-tinted, that a pessimist has at least the consolation of knowing that he has done with all illusions.

But there are as many suspect motives for seeing the world through black as through rose-coloured spectacles—the desire to forestall disillusionment, excuse failure or avoid moral responsibility, the satisfaction to one's vanity of feeling that one is hard-headed, sadism, hatred of life, the exhilaration of projecting on to the world the destructive forces in oneself. Even the fantasies of commercial entertainment are not necessarily prettier than the world from which they briefly deliver us; witness, not the brutality, but the sombre mood, harsh and sordid backgrounds, and bitter endings of American and American-style sex-and-crime novels, which have long since purged themselves of any element of reality that does not contribute directly to our enjoyment. The dangerous word 'sentimentality', with its implication that deceiving emotions are always soft and tender, leaves those who over-use it defenceless against half the emotional factors which distort judgment.

Granted that two artists see with equal clarity the obstacles to happiness, yet one affirms and the other denies, is it a matter of taste which I prefer? Whether I love or hate, trust or doubt, hope or despair, respect or despise, am happy or miserable, depends partly on the object and partly on myself. I need to see clearly the objective factors bearing on my choice; I also need the inward capacity to love or trust or be happy when the external conditions permit. A writer who undermines instead of raising this capacity is as dangerous as one who gives false grounds for the affirmative choice. If, for example, he is to persuade me that the love of humanity implicit in Maxim Gorky's *Autobiography* is sentimentality, he has the heavy task of convincing me that he sees more of human misery, cruelty and weakness than Gorki did; and if he can speak only in generalities, and lacks Gorki's power to realize concretely, his book is simply a nuisance, dangerous to me if I do not see through it.

In this sense, it is a necessary principle that it is better to affirm than to deny.[1] But it is a principle which is very easily abused. In many modern writers it is the negative passions

---

[1] Cf. part I, chapter 3.

which sound true; affirmative professions reflect, not authentic feeling, but an abstract ethic or the fear of inner emptiness. We must prefer a book in which the negative vision is genuine, and serves its purpose of exposing illusions, to one which merely pretends to affirm. Several writers, Faulkner for example, have degenerated since they took on their shoulders the burden of saying something positive. Edith Sitwell has appended happy endings to some of her darker poems, apparently from a sense of duty rather than from any deep impulse to reshape them in accordance with her personal development. Her *Gold Coast Customs* used to end 'But even the ratwhine has guttered low'; its present last line is 'For the fires of God go marching on'.

Again, much of the literature which seems most obviously 'on the side of Death' contains an element of emotional expression or wish-fulfilment fantasy which puts it beyond the reach of this or any other necessary standard. The original *Gold Coast Customs* is an exhilarating, not a depressing poem. It invites us to surrender completely but temporarily to despair; we dance on the grave of Western civilization, and feel the better for it afterwards. It does not infect us with, but briefly innoculates us against, the mood of *Gold Coast Customs*. The objection to it as a poem is not that it weakens our capacity for hope, but that after its beneficial effect wears off, it leaves too little lasting impression good or bad.

An element of morbid wish-fulfilment is an impurity in the sensibility even of poets of the stature of Webster and Baudelaire. The dark view of life becomes a voluptuous sable; we do not experience it with detachment, yet it excites instead of depressing. To the extent that this component is present, the poet's view of life becomes merely literary; we can imagine it but not live it. In imagination, impulses which in action are miserable release from more miserable tension can enter into new combinations and become positively enjoyable. Reading, I can intoxicate myself with despair, or savour the embraces of Death; but outside the book despair is the end even of the hope of enjoying despair, and death is the end of all sensation pleasant or unpleasant.

At first sight this morbidity may seem to be the ultimate sin against Life; the poet does not merely lack the power to affirm, he denies for the fun of it. But his true fault is failure of detachment, so that the necessary standards cease to apply to him. His attitude is no longer an erroneous preparation for action; it can be enjoyed in imagination only by disconnecting it from action. It is no longer even clear that he is undermining the capacity to live affirmatively; as in a crime story, there is the possibility that imaginative self-indulgence is a safety-valve.

6. MORALITY

Aesthetic valuation is the valuation of every kind of communicable experience; it is only at certain places, notably the treatment of personal relationships in the novel and drama, that it overlaps moral judgment. Except during the brief reign of 'Art for art's sake' in the nineteenth and early twentieth centuries, critics have generally agreed that moral standards are relevant within the common area. 'Art for art's sake' had the healthy effect of countering some of the absurdities of moralism in literature—the condemnation of authors who describe sexual behaviour or use four-letter words, insistence on an explicit moral and the punishment of the wicked, indifference to art which is not immediately relevant to moral issues. It will already be clear that the present theory of values excludes the absolute divorce of aesthetic from moral judgments, but there are several questions which we have still to answer. Are moral and aesthetic judgments based on different standards, so that there may be times when we must reluctantly condemn a flawless work of art as immoral? We have concluded that conflicting moral codes may be equally suited to the differing needs of individuals and communities. Does it follow that any moral judgment of a work of art is hypothetical, relative to the standards of the critic?

When we judge a book as entertainment, it is clear that moral standards may conflict with every other standard by which we value it; it may be highly enjoyable but immoral. A book is entertainment if we read it for immediate enjoyment; we are not looking for permanent benefit from it, although, as with tobacco and alcohol, we do not want lasting ill effects either. Whether it is immoral we can judge quite crudely, following the kind of procedure which condemned *Ulysses* and *Lady Chatterley*. If the hero is wicked, so is the book; if it describes torture in detail, it is sadistic. A defender of the book cannot object, as he may in the case of a serious novel, that the author's values should not be confused with those of his central character, and that cruelty is a fact of human behaviour which the author has the right to explore. The reader enjoys the adventure by identifying himself with the hero, and detachment spoils the book; the details of the torture are there for him to savour, otherwise the author would have left them out. The only remaining question is whether immoral imagination is a stimulus to, or a safety-valve which prevents immoral action—a difficult question, answerable only in relation to the kind of book and the kind of reader.

On the other hand no one can identify himself with Macbeth, or enjoy the blinding of Gloucester in *Lear*, without dislocating his experience of the play as a whole. At this level, evidently, we cannot apply moral standards so crudely; can we discard them? Suppose that I set out to judge a novel or play by purely aesthetic standards excluding moral considerations. Among these standards let us concentrate on two: the behaviour of the characters should be 'true to life', true by the fifth of our eight definitions, and the work should be an integrated whole in which the parts are mutually dependent. At first sight it may seem that the author's understanding of his characters may be separated from his moral attitude to them. But we saw in the second part of this book that subjective understanding of a person is inseparable from moral involvement. Reading, I understand the characters to the degree that I think and feel from their different points of view. Since the book is not of the kind in which I can identify myself with the hero, I feel with all the characters, and must reconcile or choose between the conflicting inclinations not of one but of all. My attitude to each therefore modifies my attitude to all

I

the rest; and this is one aspect of the book's aesthetic organization, within which each part contributes to the whole.

But all this is another way of saying that although I can judge egoistically where the hero is my idealized self, here I judge altruistically. If the author is morally unjust to a character, he has failed to evoke him as a living presence, or his attitudes to different characters are badly articulated, or malice has broken the detachment of the novel. If a character is lifeless, unrealized, the moral issue is unreal; if he is enigmatic, his motives deliberately hidden, the author is morally uncommitted. Kafka's novels may serve as a limiting case; one character is surrounded by unreadable faces, and there is no fixed moral attitude, only the exploration of moral doubt.

Suppose that I object morally to Proust's treatment of love. A woman who is loved, Albertine, Rachel or Odette, is simply a thing, which the lover strives vainly to possess by bribes, lies and threats; women assume personality only when they are not loved—Mme Verdurin, Mme de Villeparisis, Mme de Guermantes, Françoise. Without positively recommending this attitude, Proust assumes that love is a need too desperate for any moral quibbling; it is an irreclaimable chaos which can never be brought within the moral order. Saying this am I merely judging by standards which others may not share? The moral objection that Albertine, for example, is not treated as a person is the aesthetic objection that she is not realized as a character. Proust's characters are real to the extent that they are voices, and we do not hear Albertine or even Odette talking. As soon as a character in Proust loves, the object is hidden from him, and from Proust, by his intense preoccupation with his own emotions. There is no interaction between man and woman, only the reaction of the man. However brilliantly Proust reveals from one side the love, anxious, possessive, jealous, self-centred, which for him is Love in general, he always seems to know only half of what is going on. He sees that jealousy is suffering, but not that it is infliction of suffering; he knows that the man is trying to force love out of the woman, but seems only half aware that the force is driving her further away.

The husband in *Anna Karenina* is superficially very like the traditional cuckold of comedies of adultery. Could a writer present Karenin exactly as Tolstoy shows him, yet invite us to regard him simply as a ridiculous and morally irrelevant obstacle to the lovers? I see the traditional wronged husband mostly from outside; the author invites me to identify myself with Don Juan, and if he ever allows me to *feel* the husband's humiliation, it is to gratify my male vanity. If Tolstoy is more charitable, it is not because his deeper exploration reveals the husband as more attractive inside than outside; on the contrary, he exposes him much more ruthlessly. Loss of face and interference with his routine hurt Karenin much more than his betrayed feelings; he never understands that his own failure as a husband is a cause of the disaster; his forgiveness when he believes Anna is dying, genuine for a moment, changes into a device for escaping his humiliation by dramatizing himself as a saint. Tolstoy never tells me that I ought to sympathize with Karenin, scarcely offers a hint to guide me towards sympathy; he simply presents the man and his actions, the effects of his actions on others and of theirs on him. But he refuses to let me judge Karenin from Vronsky's point of view; he insists that I stand equally near to both of them, share the experience of a stunted person fumbling to extricate himself from a misery which he cannot understand, and recognize that his inability to love makes his misery not less but greater. Vronsky himself, who at first took the conventional idea of the ridiculous husband for granted, lost it as soon as he met Karenin face to face.

For D. H. Lawrence, suffering has no moral significance and is disgusting rather than moving. He has an immediate sympathy for anything which is alive, and revulsion from anything dead; but he does not pity. Christians consider pity a virtue, La Rochefoucauld and Nietzsche did not; shall we say simply that Lawrence is right by some standards and wrong by others? No, for the statement that he is not compassionate, nor cruel either, although he is sometimes vindictive, is another way of saying that his characters do not suffer. (Contrast Lady Chatterley's husband with Anna Karenina's.) An important fact of experience is outside his range as a writer. When suffering does intrude into a novel, for example Somers' wartime miseries in Cornwall, in *Kangaroo*, we sense at once that it is the author's own, and that he is seeing it out of proportion.

Standards of conduct are relative, according to the present theory of morals; but particular actions are right or wrong for any observer, who should judge them in relation to the ends of those affected and to their fitness as means. A writer can present a self-contained world in which the reader knows all the relevant motives and circumstances of an action, and in which, even if there is no explicit moral comment, only one moral attitude is possible, unless standards are imported from outside. For author and reader alike the novel is a moral exploration, in which standards of conduct, like other theorectical principles used in the construction of the work, are guides to be discarded as soon as they contradict his spontaneous sympathy or antipathy for an action seen in relation to its motives and circumstances. The enterprise succeeds only if the writer allows the work to take shape in accordance with its own laws, whether or not it confirms his moral preconceptions; even if he tries to formulate his conclusions in an explicit moral, he often simplifies, indeed betrays, his own vision (cf. 'Vengeance is mine, I will repay' under the title of *Anna Karenina*).

If Lawrence's novels influence me morally, it is not by infecting me with his own powerful emotions. If, for example, he alters my sexual morality, it is by showing me people whose affirmative possibilities are intimately connected, by interrelations which I have never before recognized in myself, with the sexual impulse, and are diminished by its repression, its impoverishment as sensuality, and its intellectualization as a concept of Love. Since I cannot doubt the necessary principle that it is better to live affirmatively than negatively, I cannot accept his account of these people without accepting his valuation of them, and I cannot recognize their similarity to myself without revising my own moral standards.

The principle that a work of art ought not to have an explicit moral is a technical maxim, of course like all such maxims liable to exceptions. A novel or play can value the actions of particular characters in particular situations, but cannot justify a universal moral principle. In any case if the moral is implicit in the story it is unnecessary to state it openly, and if it is not implicit in the story, the writer has given us no grounds for accepting it; either he is guilty of the impertinence of expecting us to take his word for it, or, worse still, deludes us into accepting it by an appeal to our emotions.

The morality inherent in the organization of a 'novel', if we confine this name to stories which exclude the supernatural, is purely humanistic. A novelist can demonstrate only that an action is compatible or incompatible with the happiness of his characters in the situation he presents. If, for example, he is a Catholic, and believes that divorce and birth control are wrong even when they contribute to earthly happiness, he must import these standards from outside. The present argument will therefore be irrelevant for him; he must hold that a work may be aesthetically good but immoral, or good in every respect except that it is immoral. On the other hand, absolute standards may be inherent in a work like Marlowe's *Faustus*, in which the Devil is a character and damnation an event. In this case we accept Marlowe's judgment of the man he presents in the circumstances he presents; but whether we think that such circumstances exist outside the play, whether we are committed to a similar judgment of Faustian conduct in ordinary life, depends on our theological beliefs.

Personal relationships are not the only area in which moral and aesthetic judgments coincide. The Greeks and the Chinese attached a moral significance to music which many people nowadays find scarcely intelligible. Jazz is the only contemporary music which affects us at all similarly, as a force which might disintegrate or revitalize the social order. A person listening to jazz relaxes and enjoys his heightened spontaneity, welcoming the release from inhibitions; or he resists it as a temptation to slacken self-control and be swept away into chaos; or he sits rigidly, with a tensed face and twitching mouth, savouring it as though it were pornography. Whether he is exhilarated by the success of its improvized figures or disgusted by its looseness of form, whether he prefers Dionysus or Apollo, depends on his moral trust or mistrust of the uncontrollable. Thought and control are good when they prevent disintegration (keeping one's head in a panic), bad when they inhibit spontaneous integration (the tightrope-walker thinking what to do next). The aesthetic judgment that the notes spontaneously assume satisfying patterns is at the same time the moral judgment that in this case the suspension of control is right, that instead of allowing impulses to conflict it enables them to reintegrate in a new order. The aesthetic judgment that the music is shapeless and discordant, that it needs the discipline of written composition, is at the same time a denial of this moral claim.

7. DETACHMENT

Reading a certain kind of story for amusement, I give my sympathies directly to the hero and against the villain, want the hero to win and will be disappointed—and astonished—if he does not. I am willing to suffer a little, but in the knowledge that the fear and disappointment of present danger and failure will only increase the joy of eventual escape and success; the function of the book is to entertain me. But the kind of writer who is called an artist does not seem to care whether or not he disappoints my hopes. His story follows its own logic, ignoring my likes and dislikes, to the appropriate ending which may or may not be happy, damnation for Marlowe's Faust, salvation for Goethe's. This 'detachment' or 'impersonality' is not a refusal to suffer with his characters; their sensations, pleasant and unpleasant, are much more distinct and vivid than those evoked by the story I read for amusement. Why then should I gratuitously make myself suffer by putting myself at the mercy of an author who refuses to manipulate the story in accordance with my sympathies?

A preliminary answer, which only raises the question again in a different form, is that the more I suffer with King Lear the more I enjoy the play. By casting my bread on the waters, and following Lear to madness and death, I win a just but unexpected reward; ceasing to care whether I enjoy or not, I enjoy more deeply. Indeed, there is no kind of art which requires me to discard entirely the hedonist test I apply to entertainment. If I am forced to admit that an acknowledged classic bores me or depresses me, the failure to enjoy is a warning, either that I have misunderstood it, or that the work is finally unsuccessful, however many the abstract reasons for admiring it.

Outside the arts I can achieve a similar detachment towards the experiences of people with whom I have no personal ties, in biographies and memoirs for example, and a partial detachment towards even my own past experiences. When I recall the past, I may behave as I do when reading for amusement, dwelling on pleasant and shrinking from unpleasant memories. But if I wish to understand a past event in my life, discover why it happened, where I went wrong, how it looks in the eyes of other people, I must be detached, recalling its painful and humiliating as unflinchingly as its pleasant aspects. The renewal of an unpleasant emotion is still unpleasant, but it has changed its character; the more precisely I recall how miserable I felt, the more the recollection contributes to the achievement of a new aim, understanding.

Detachment is inhibition of the tendency to welcome the pleasant and shrink from the unpleasant. If a writer is seeking to entertain us for a moment, detachment is obviously a vice for him; he needs it, however, if his aim is to help us to understand how to live and to act. But why is it that we enjoy his instruction, never feel 'This hurts but it is good for me'? Because in the experience of a work of art we function mentally beyond our usual capacity, think, imagine and feel more variously and yet more harmoniously than in ordinary life, more spontaneously, with more distinct and vivid sensations and richer emotional associations, free from the prejudices and self-deceptions which distort insight, entering more easily and fully into the minds of others, responding more affirmatively, appraising morally with more sensitivity. The joy may be compared with that of good health when we are positively aware of it, in convalescence or after physical exertion, or to the satisfaction of a task or a game which gives more than usual opportunities to exercise our skill.

Detachment, as we have seen, is not a refusal to feel. Whenever a writer impresses us as coldly, frigidly, clinically impersonal, there is reason to suspect that he is not detached at all. If he is really observing without feeling, his characters will become automata. If the book nevertheless lives, the chances are that it is a wish-fulfilment fantasy, gratifying misanthropy or contempt, offering the consoling illusion of being emotionally invulnerable, flattering our vanity as Olympian observers of the human ant-hill.

Again, detachment is not withdrawal from action. The purpose of recalling past experience with detachment, making no distinction between pleasant and unpleasant, is to act more successfully in future. A scientist works impersonally, accepting results on their objective merits whether or not they please him, because to reject against the evidence a conclusion which disappoints him would make his results misleading as guides to action. Detachment, by the present definition, is not the same as the 'disinterested vision' discussed under the heading *Sensuousness*. The latter does involve the transformation of things from tools of action into objects to be contemplated for their own sake. We might even say, although this is a risky way of putting it, that its value implies that one kind of contemplation is superior to action; the value of action begins with its own suspension and the enjoyment of its fruits. However, this does not discredit action, merely reminds us to make it fruitful. Whether art can serve as propaganda for particular courses of action will concern us in the next chapter.

Detachment is the main criterion for distinguishing art from entertainment. In art it is necessarily good, both because it enhances the capacity to withdraw from experience in order to understand it, and because the work can be good by other necessary standards only to the extent that it is impersonal. In entertainment, on the other hand, detachment is a reduction of enjoyment, and the standards which we are considering are relevant only in the way that lung cancer is relevant to smoking; we do not want to pay for amusement by actually reducing our fitness for life. However, inhibition of the tendency to shrink from unpleasant experience is a matter of degree. Apart from the wide central belt of successful compromises between the demands of art and entertainment, the works which ask to be judged by necessary standards are detached only in varying degrees. Granted that emotional gratification is an impurity at this level, it is only one of many possible vices, and the purest art, it is widely agreed, is not always the best.

Within the Elizabethan and Jacobean drama, are Webster's tragedies truly impersonal? We can say only that they are more so than Tourneur's, less so than Shakespeare's. His vision of the destructive forces in man is perhaps the most intense in English literature, but he is attracted as well as repelled. His sense of evil is too voluptuous, and his obsession with the misery of the human condition outlasts its usefulness within the play, so that afterwards the spectator is not sure that he has quite emerged from the 'shadow, or deep pit of darkness' where 'womanish and fearful mankind' lives, nor even that he altogether wants to. But clearly this does not imply that Webster's plays, or Tourneur's for that matter, are to be judged as entertainment; we can distinguish degrees of detachment within the plays of Shakespeare himself. In contrast with *Antony and Cleopatra, Romeo and Juliet* is partly shaped by the death-wish hidden in romantic love; if Friar Lawrence had come in time the lovers might have lived happily ever after, and the artificial turn of the plot is a sign that they die because we want them to die.

At this point let us take a second look at the questions we dismissed at the beginning of the discussion: 'What is art?', 'What is the aesthetic quality?' When someone asks whether a detective story by Georges Simenon or Raymond Chandler should be judged as literature or merely enjoyed as entertainment, he is asking a real question. He is right in assuming that a work classed as literature is good or bad in itself, however much critics disagree over it. The mistake is to suppose that this way of talking implies the presence in the work of an aesthetic quality which the imperceptive fail to see. The point is not that the value is in the work, but that the standards by which it is approved are necessary. This change of viewpoint has a great advantage; there is no longer any need to look for a single quality, and no reason to suppose that there is only one standard. The discovery of the aesthetic quality, whenever it has any relevance at all to criticism of the arts, always results in the elevation of one standard at the expense of others. If the essence of beauty is 'Unity within Variety', we must judge the experience of a work of art *solely* by the degree to which it is at once varied and unified, and therefore exclude from art everything which satisfies other standards equally necessary—in other words, we must limit the name 'art' to part only of the work which is good in itself.

II

HYPOTHETICAL JUDGMENTS

WE VALUE a work hypothetically when we judge it in relation to the needs of a particular individual or society, time or place. John Osborne's *Look Back in Anger* is among the important plays of the 1950s. Why? Because it is the first to put on the stage certain human types which have emerged since 1945. Will that matter a hundred years from today? Is it a good play *sub specie aeternitatis*? Very likely not; but even if it will not help people of other times and places to understand their situation, it does help us.

Hypothetical appraisals, although relative to particular needs, are based on objective grounds; they are not to be confused with recommendations in terms of subjective tastes. In the case of *Look Back in Anger*, the recommendation is addressed to people who live in mid-century England and are involved in its problems, not to people who have a weakness for plays on contemporary themes as they might have for costume melodrama or intimate revue. The subjective tastes which govern our choice of entertainment of course affect aesthetic judgments, but only by distorting them. The worth of Conrad's novels or of *Anna Karenina* has nothing to do with a taste for sea-stories or love-stories.

X likes documentary realism, Y responds more easily the more radically an artist transforms brute fact; X likes the hard and lucid, Y the vague and evocative; X likes the reasonable, Y the irrational image which works without him knowing how. Either of them may well offer us his prejudices in the form of a standard, affirming that art *ought* to be hard and distinct, with

firm outlines, or that art is worthless unless we can sense in it
something just beyond our reach. But what reason can be
given for such standards, unless it is that principle which we all
in varying degrees confuse with the categorical imperative,
'You ought to be like me'? Everyone who attains a certain
degree of self-consciousness knows that he has temperamental
preferences and blind spots which affect his capacity to
appreciate different kinds of art. As his taste develops the blind
spots diminish, but he can never hope to reach a perfection
which enables him to judge every work with equal confidence.
He learns to make his subjective tastes explicit, so that others
can discount his bias while listening to his opinions.

The extreme case of political propaganda makes a convenient point from which to attack the problem of hypothetical
standards. A novelist, let us say, makes us feel intensely the
misery of the workers in a capitalist society, and shows us the
Communists helping them: moral, 'Join the Communists'. But
the conclusion does not follow from what he shows us.
Whether the Marxist solution will in fact cure the ills of the
proletariat, and how far Communist practice accords with
Marxist theory, involve complicated questions of politics and
economics which the writer cannot discuss at length even in a
novel as vast and loosely constructed as *War and Peace*.
Picasso's *Guernica* circulated during the Spanish civil war as
propaganda against Fascism. But what evidence can a painting
give that it is only Fascists who bomb women and children?
Or that in the conditions of modern warfare it is possible to
fight for any cause without doing so? As a matter of fact we
now know that the assumptions of the painting as propaganda
are wrong on both counts. Within a few years the destruction
of cities from the air proved to be a specifically Anglo-
American weapon; the Nazis were less interested in it, because
of a different estimate of the relative importance of air and
land warfare. These prosaic facts have nothing to do with the
value of *Guernica* as a painting, but a great deal to do with
its function as propaganda. Anyone who allowed it to
affect his political sympathies was deceived, and deceived
himself.

An aversion to propaganda in the arts does not imply that one has retreated into the ivory tower, or that one denies that the artist's opinions may be acceptable on other grounds. The point is simply that if he seeks to convert us to his beliefs, without being able to give his evidence because of the limitations of his medium, he can convert us only by working on our emotions. Responding to a work of art, we allow the artist, indeed help him by our active co-operation, to stimulate us as he pleases; unless we hold on to the right to judge his effects for ourselves, we are surrendering to a hypnotist, without knowing whether he is benefiting or harming us. If effective propaganda is good art, then it is good to let others manipulate our judgment for their own ends.

Ignoring the Communist writer's moral, may we not still learn important truths from him, about the nature of class conflicts for example, or the sensations of an unemployed man with a family to support? It is clear that in practice we do pick up a great deal of information about social problems from novels, plays and films, and that in doing so we are not always passively allowing ourselves to be infected with the author's opinions. Suppose that I am reading a novel about conflict between whites and nationalists in a British colony. I have always believed that the natives are savages unfit to govern themselves, and that the British took over the country reluctantly in order to save them from the misrule of their Sultan; I am a little hurt by their ingratitude in listening to the promises of irresponsible agitators in the pay of a foreign power. As I read, my opinions alter; it begins to seem to me that the British are in the country primarily for the mines, the copra and the value of its main harbour as a naval base; that, although they recognize responsibilities to their subjects and have done them a great deal of good, they would not remove any injustice at the cost of damaging these interests; that actions which from above are legitimate defence of these interests are oppression seen from below; that it is by no means a simple question whether the civilization of these people is inferior to our own; that a master concerned primarily with his own interests cannot expect gratitude from his servants even for real benefits, and that nationalism is intimately connected with the self-respect of the people.

But how has the book affected me? Certainly not by providing new information about the colony. If the writer tries to rouse my anger by crediting his British administrators with corruption or atrocities of a kind which I have never seen reported in any British colony, my belief in the story is at once suspended; at best I keep the accusation in mind as a point worth checking. A journalist can tell us what he has seen, and give evidence for what he reports at second hand; but a novelist, even if he has seen as much, renounces his authority as an eye-witness by presenting his experience as fiction. For all I can tell by the novel alone, there may not be any movement for independence in this particular country, there may not be any such country. Perhaps the writer is interested in types of personality and behaviour which come into the open in revolutionary situations, and this colony is merely a symbol through which he explores them.

The book works on me by increasing my subjective understanding of objective facts. I know the facts already in the abstract, but without putting myself in the place either of the colonial settlers and officials or of the nationalists. As soon as I do so, I begin to see through my moral simplifications. I have credited the British with a disinterested benevolence which seems hardly likely once I seriously imagine myself in their situation; I have accepted the superiority of my own customs without considering why they should seem superior to people brought up in other customs; I have demanded a gratitude which I should not feel myself in the position of the nationalists. My estimate of the relative weight of economic interest and moral principle for the rulers, and of the material benefits and the humiliations of alien government for the subjects, changes drastically as soon as I look at the conflict from near to and from both sides.

What if the writer presents, side by side with Englishmen who are a convincing mixture of selfishness and good intentions, nationalists who are incorruptible heroes fighting for the liberty of their people? The book does not lose its significance as a one-sided subjective interpretation, of the same interest as a cogent but partisan selection of objective arguments. On the other hand if I am reading the book in order to clarify my ideas and feelings about imperialism and anti-imperialism, its value for me will be much less if it prevents me subjectively understanding the nationalists as well as the whites. The writer ought, even against the grain of his prejudices, to turn the nationalist leaders into intelligible human beings by showing that the appetites for power, gain and revenge are entangled with their patriotism; that a government in their hands will be much more corrupt than that of the British, and their methods of fighting more barbarous; and that although the nationalist minority claims to, and up to a point does, represent the people, the people have only the vaguest sympathy with it except when a crisis directly touches their standard of living. This sharing of the author's sympathies and antipathies between the two sides will not necessarily prevent him from committing himself to one or the other. If he does, we can still call the book propaganda if we choose, but not in the pejorative sense of the word. It will have lost its emotive force for readers who like clear and simple issues, but those whom it persuades will have convictions which do not depend on inhibiting imagination and ignoring facts.

The hypothetical value of the novel depends on its authenticity as a record of the life of the colony. But the situation within the novel illuminates the situation in the colony only to the extent that the writer's attitude to the former is good by *necessary* standards. He increases my understanding, even on the political level, only if he achieves a varied and finely integrated attitude (helping me, for example, to reconcile sympathy with the wounded self-respect of subject peoples, and aversion from the mixture of pride and servility which it causes, two reactions which previously seemed to me mutually exclusive), evokes the landscape and people with sensuous vividness and clarity, understands from within characters on both sides of the conflict, realistically acknowledges facts which are counter to his sympathies, is sensitive to the moral issues involved in political conflicts. The value of the book as a document will last only as long as the political issue which it reflects; sooner or later the novelist's imagined world will be judged as an isolated and self-contained construction, and will satisfy necessary tests alone or be forgotten. An attitude good enough to illuminate a particular problem may not be good enough to survive as a criticism of life. But the novelist is not faced with a choice between necessary and hypothetical value, writing for posterity and writing for his contemporaries. The more successfully he interprets his particular situation, the better he is writing by necessary standards.

Although the documentary novelist is an extreme case, every artist has his particular needs which may or may not be similar to ours; the harmony which he seeks is the resolution of conflicts peculiar to himself, the reality to which he must adapt himself consists of specific and local facts. From the point of view of Yeats, to take an example far removed from our political novelist, harmony is accord between his spiritual and physical desires, openly in conflict in his *Dialogue of Self and Soul*, variously and momentarily reconciled in poems as unlike as *Byzantium*, *Leda and the Swan*, and *Crazy Jane*: reality is his own decrepitude in old age, 'Whiggery', the revival of political violence, the breakdown of a civilized tradition. Similarly, every reader has his own needs, and seeks out the writers who can help him to the solution of problems on every level from the discovery of a personal philosophy to the understanding of juvenile delinquency. He is not, of course, bound to prefer them to others who do not immediately touch his personal needs; in the last resort he gains more from writers who in some vague way illuminate 'life', who enhance his general capacity to think, feel and sense, than from those who make quite specific contributions to the understanding of the relation of the individual to society, the meaning of Stalin's purges, the degeneration of mass culture, or whatever concerns him at the moment. But contemporary literature, and older literature which happens to coincide with our preoccupations, are bound to have an importance for us out of all proportion to their value by necessary standards. It would be absurd to refuse all but the most general benefits from the arts. For the present Kafka helps us to understand our situation; if readers of the future are baffled by our interest in this madman, so much the better for them.

It used to be held that great art is eternal because it interprets universal themes, not the transitory concerns of a particular time and place. No doubt it is true that generality of theme has something to do with breadth and persistence of appeal. But it is no longer possible, in a time of accelerating change and increasing knowledge of other civilizations, to imagine that universality is absolute or has anything to do with the necessary value of a work of art. Yeats' conflict between soul and flesh belongs to Europe and Western Asia; it underlies his *Dialogue of Self and Soul*, and Villon's *Debat du cuer et du corps*, but not T'ao Ch'ien's *Substance, Shadow and Spirit* (in Arthur Waley's *One Hunderd and Seventy Chinese Poems*). His concern with the physical degeneration of old age he no doubt shares with everyone up to the twentieth century who has lived out his natural span; a little further advance in biology, and it may not last into the twenty-first. The merry month of May, and the quick passing of youth and beauty, have lost most of their significance in the seasonless life of the modern city, where women no longer lose their beauty soon after twenty. Love, in the wide sense of an affection not confined to lust, is fairly widespread, but the special meaning of the word for Europeans is not older than the Troubadours. The four seasons are a universal theme within the Temperate Zone; the loosening of the family has dislodged incest from the esteem it kept in the eyes of poets from Sophocles to Byron; within a few years everything written about the moon may have the oddity of Donne's 'Oh my America! my new-found-land'.

K

PART IV

Science and Myth

12

MYTHICAL AND METAPHYSICAL WORLD-PICTURES

THE only kind of language which matters is language which describes something; this was the unspoken assumption of the men who developed those standards which we now accept, or violently repudiate, or unwillingly relinquish, and it still hinders us when we struggle to achieve new standards or new reasons for the old ones. Scientists tell us about one kind of reality, philosophers, prophets, moralists and poets tell us about spiritual entities which are equally if not more real, goodness, truth and beauty, the soul, God. Unless this is so, unless actions and things are objectively good and beautiful, and there is a soul in me which recognizes these qualities imperceptible to my senses, what grounds can there be for choosing between one course of action and another? The same preconception, that words are discredited if we can find no things corresponding to them, affects those who reject this celestial apparatus; they tend to conclude that life is meaningless, or that they can now do as they like, or that they must somehow deduce a way of living from the descriptive propositions of science.

It once seemed that everywhere in the material world one could discern evidence of the spiritual reality behind it. How did the universe begin if there is no Creator? How can mechanical cause and effect account for the emergence of life in inorganic matter, the emergence of mind in the unthinking animal? Are there not unmistakable signs of a designing intelligence and a guiding purpose in nature, and indisputable records of divine intervention in history? How can we explain the behaviour of a human being, who is more than a machine or a physical system, without assuming a directing mind, a mind which in any case is apparent to introspection? But since the seventeenth century scientists have been busy filling one after the other the gaps in the physical world where spirit seemed to show through. Newton established the ground plan of an explanation of nature in terms of cause and effect, excluding purpose; Darwin extended the explanation from the inanimate to the animate. Kant demolished the classical arguments for the existence of God; the Higher Criticism disposed of the historical evidence of divine intervention; biologists, neurologists and psychologists have gradually undermined the assumption that the emergence of life and mind require special explanations. The better we understand the material world, the less reason we find to suppose there is any other; the more science adds to the means of controlling man's environment, the harder it becomes to justify the ends which they serve.

Anyone who assumes a God who is First Cause of physical events, or a mind which interacts with the body, is at bottom, however convinced he may be that he has liberated himself from such crude analogies, conceiving the spiritual as a kind of ether too fine even to transmit light waves; and it has become more and more plain that this entity, like the ether of nine-teenth-century physics, systematically eludes search. We must make an absolute distinction between the kinds of evidence on which we accept statements about matter and statements about spirit. Scientists reason from the data of sense experience, and can discern no trace of spirit, values, God. We know, however, that these entities are as real as the things we see and hear, because . . . because we need them, we cannot live without them. If there is no longer any hope of proving their existence (or subsistence, if you prefer), at least we have the consolation that they are now beyond the reach of scientific refutation. Drawing confidence from this invulnerability, we may even speak condescendingly of the limitations of science, which uses instruments too crude to discern these important entities, and smile indulgently at the bearded Victorians who imagined that there is an irreconcilable conflict between Science and Religion.

But the trouble with this solution is that it seems impossible to draw the dividing line with the consistency needed to keep spirit entirely out of reach of the coarse fingers of scientists. There remains one place where spirit and matter meet, the interaction of mind and body, and a behaviourist psychology can still dislodge spirit from its last foothold in the material world. Even those whom behaviourism most repels must find it hard to resist a foreboding of its victory. We know by long experience that whenever science clashes with our finer feelings over the explanation of a fact, it is our finer feelings which are wrong.

Suppose that I try to dispense with these untraceable entities; where does that leave me? The 'neutralization of nature', the draining of all significance out of the universe, reached its limit in nineteenth-century materialism. The peculiarity of materialism is that it allows no possibility of finding grounds for any kind of action, even for resigning myself to the meaninglessness of life and doing as I please in the knowledge that one course of action is no better nor worse than another. It eliminates God, the mind, goodness, even pleasure, and at the same time implies that I can have no use for such concepts anyway. It ought not to matter to me that there are no grounds for choice, because in any case I cannot choose; I am a collection of atoms following a predetermined course like the planets. There is no 'meaning' or 'purpose' in the universe, only atoms obeying natural laws; but neither can there be any yearning for meaning and purpose in me, only natural processes in my nervous system. Abolishing values, materialism also abolishes the problem of values. Yet somehow here I still am, needing to choose although my actions are predetermined, uneasy at the loss of values which are no more conceivable as factors in neural disturbances than as qualities of matter, translating everything which the materialists say into an account of a positively alien, inhuman, hostile, merciless world as remote from their dispassionate intentions as the benevolent universe of Christianity is. Since there are no values by which to choose, and the choice is in any case an illusion, shall I simply give up pretending to choose, and watch passively as my body goes through its causally determined motions? But then my body falls into inertia. Moreover, even withdrawal from choice implies an 'I' distinct from my body, which is incompatible with materialism. Everything can be explained in terms of cause and effect, even my own behaviour up to this moment; but among those mysterious entities the existence of which materialism denies, by the side of God, goodness, beauty and pleasure, is myself as I am now. The fault which Kierkegaard found in all systems is most visible in materialism: 'There must be no existing remainder, not even such a little minikin as the existing Herr Professor who writes the system.'

The twentieth-century shift of attention from things to words seemed at first to confirm the neutralization of nature. Materialists had assumed that all religions, and all metaphysical systems except their own, describe wrongly what science describes rightly. But exploration of the functions of language soon showed that the indicative mood and regular word-order are no guarantee that a sentence has the function of conveying information. The kind of language which describes an object, or which requires, permits or forbids descriptive statements about an object, contracted until scarcely anything remained except science, logic and mathematics. The kind of language which proposes action and excites emotion, which formerly seemed to be safely confined within the imperative mood and interrogative and exclamatory sentence patterns, swelled until it included the whole of religion, metaphysics, morals and literature. The Logical Positivists, retaining the traditional assumption that language is meaningful only when it conveys information, took verifiability by sense experience as the test of meaning. It seemed to follow that the language which professes to answer such questions as 'What shall I do?', 'How shall I live?' is not false but meaningless. At the time when we seem to be saying the most, we are saying nothing at all.

But linguistic philosophy is not an end but a turning point; if it confirms that there are no values, it also implies that in treating values as entities we were seeing the problem from a wrong point of view. No modern philosophy has excited such fierce reactions in the broad masses of the intelligentsia as the Logical Positivism imported by Ayer in the 1930s, iconoclastic joy in those who were positivist by temperament, mingled fear and contempt in those who were not. But both parties assumed that language is degraded by denying that it is descriptive, and did not notice that this is only another of the traditional assumptions which Logical Positivism itself discredits. They mistook the frontier between different uses of language for a boundary drawn around the only language which matters. But when the scope of descriptive language narrows to exclude the whole of metaphysics, religion and literature, and all the language in which we ask questions, make decisions and give moral, prudential and technical advice, from the Sermon on the Mount to instructions how to drive a car, it becomes clear that the first consequence of the revolution is to dislodge descriptive language from its old pre-eminence. A person who uses only language verifiable by sense experience could report a past action ('I took the turning to the left'), but before the event he could not ask what to do ('Which way shall I go?'), understand instructions ('Turn left') or decide ('I will turn left'). He would be a camera eye, watching the world without living in it.

This brings us again to the dilemma of living by a materialist philosophy, and at once resolves it. When we turn back from the object to the language in which we talk about the object, the impossibility of living in the world described by science becomes the impossibility of living without using language for other purposes besides description. Scientists have not discovered a neutral universe, but learned to describe the universe in neutral language. Their account tantalizes us with the suspicion that it leaves out an indefinable X more important than everything it includes, the feeling of life, consciousness, force, value, purpose, significance. This X is indeed an important criterion, but it confirms the scientific account instead of discrediting it; any account which includes this X can be rejected out of hand, because to the extent that the account evokes feeling it is not a pure description. The accusation that the limitations of science prevent it from discovering values, which are so much more important than its gross material facts, becomes the tautology that scientific language, since to be scientific it must be devoid of prescriptive and emotive implications, cannot prescribe, express or evoke.

To be disillusioned by the neutral universe of science, and conclude that life is without purpose, is as though I were to set out to analyse a game which I enjoy playing, discover with growing alarm that I can find no trace of any quality of being interesting, exciting or entertaining, and conclude that it must be dull. 'It is interesting', 'It is dull' are expressions of interest and boredom; they have no place in any description of the game, although 'He is interested', 'He is bored' have a place in a description of the players. Similarly, 'Life has a purpose', 'Life has no purpose' express faith and disillusionment; we cannot expect to find any quality of value or purpose in a description of the universe, only an account of the purposeful or purposeless behaviour of the speaker.

In order to understand myself and my situation, I need to describe; in order to act in relation to my situation, I need to ask questions, make decisions, give and take advice, control and modify my emotions. The terms 'true' and 'false' do not apply to inquiry, decision, advice and expression of emotion, although they do apply to descriptions of these activities. The mere objection that it is neither true nor false is irrelevant to any language which guides emotion and action, from the recipés in a cookery book to the Apostles' Creed. When Logical Positivists, instead of raising objections to the existence of God in the manner of earlier rationalists, claimed that 'God exists' is an assertion which conveys no information whatever, they seemed to be delivering the *coup de grâce* to theism. But the criticism amounts to saying that a theistic doctrine, instead of making a false addition to the information of science, directs its believers towards a way of life. That is exactly what such a doctrine is for; it is designed to answer the question 'How shall I live?', and to fulfil this purpose it cannot be descriptive, it must be of the same order as the language in which we advise and decide. A theistic doctrine may of course include vulnerable statements of fact, and in Christianity, for example, these are so important that few believers would be satisfied with this kind of defence. But if it does include such statements, the doctrine lays itself open to objection *because* it trespasses on the descriptive function of language by conveying information.

The disappearance of spiritual entities seems at first to leave an unfilled gap between the words and the emotions and actions which they evoke. In the case of moral and aesthetic judgments, we have already seen that this first impression is misleading. 'X is good' does not give us information about X which obliges us to approve it, but merely recommends us to approve it. We tend to assume that we approve X *because* it is good, and that approval becomes a matter of subjective choice once it is denied that value is objectively present in the action or thing. But if I can find no criteria by which to establish its presence, and to judge between my intuition of its presence and the conflicting intuitions of others, then my valuation is already a matter of subjective choice. The mere privilege of being able to speak of values as qualities, and use such consoling words as 'true' and 'real', gives no more than an illusory feeling of security. On the other hand, if I recommend X in relation to objective standards, my choice ceases to be subjective whether value is assumed to be present in X or not.

To justify value judgments, we do not need to prove that values are as real as the objects of scientific inquiry; we must show that the standards by which we evaluate are as objective as the criteria by which scientists judge questions of fact. The dilemma presented by the scientists' expulsion of value and purpose from the universe thus turns out to be a false dilemma. I. A. Richards made this point long ago, in *Principles of Literary Criticism* (1924) and *Science and Poetry* (1926), and proposed a system of standards based on a psychological theory of values. The revolution in philosophy discredited psychological theories of values at an early stage, and Richards' explanation of the relation between science and poetry has gone out of fashion. But for anyone who accepts the present theory of morals and aesthetics, his case recovers all its force.

According to the Logical Positivists of a generation ago, the analytic propositions of logic and mathematics, and the empirically verifiable propositions of science, are meaningful; other kinds of language are meaningless and cannot be either true or false. There is little point in arguing over the Logical Positivist definitions of 'meaning' and 'truth', which are no longer current in any case. The distinction between different uses of language remains valid; but whether we confine 'meaning' and 'truth' to one kind of language or extend them to all is an unimportant question of terminology. 'Did he go?', 'Go!' and 'I will go' are sentences which retain their functions unaltered whether or not we choose to class these functions under the heading 'meaning'. We do not ordinarily apply the words 'true' and 'false' to the first two sentences, and apply them to the last only if we fail to distinguish the decision from the predictions 'I shall go', so that in their case confinement to descriptive language has more justification in ordinary usage.

The golden word 'Truth' is among the most highly emotive in Western philosophy, and all other kinds of language seem to lose their efficacy if we are allowed to breathe this incantation over science alone. But it is essential not to phrase the conclusions of the Logical Positivists in just those terms which their work discredited, and accuse them of claiming to have *discovered* that a sentence is true or false only of it is empirically verifiable, and that religion and metaphysics are really meaningless. Their thesis would remain the same if we turned it inside out. We could say that the primary function of language is to make us sense, feel and act; it also has a secondary, utilitarian, function of explaining and predicting sensations, emotions and actions. Language is meaningful when it excites us to imagine an object or think, feel and intend in an imagined situation; it is true when it makes us imagine the object as we should in fact see it, and think, feel and intend as we should do in the actual situation. A novelist's account of a person may be true or false, but a behaviourist psychologist's is meaningless since it does not enable us to visualize the person or feel as he feels; it can only be useful or misleading as a guide to the way his gestures will look to us and his voice sound to us in different situations. This reversal of the thesis would detach the valid constituent in the claim that poetry gives a more direct insight into Reality than science does; describing takes us one step further from immediate experience than does the language which evokes it directly, and laws guiding the inference of descriptive statements withdraw us further still. The alteration of a few key words would have scared away half the camp following of Logical Positivism and attracted to it half of its bitterest enemies. The sense of loss when a change of definitions deprives us of the right to say 'meaning', 'reality' or 'truth' is like the indignation of the people who thought that a reform of the calendar had shortened their lives.

From the present point of view, criticism of a religion or philosophy of life is in the first place criticism of a way of feeling and acting, controlled and organized by emotive speech and gesture. (Gesture is only a little less important than speech, as in emotional communication generally—the ritual and devotional exercises of a religion, the etiquette of a social group. A common ritual is almost as necessary to hold together a religious community as common dogmas, and an adolescent rebel finds it nearly impossible to throw off the ideas of his class without also flouting its manners.) I must choose my beliefs by the necessary and hypothetical standards which govern other kinds of choice. Among these standards there is one which does make contact with scientific fact; my *Weltanschauung* ought to 'face facts', ought to be true in the seventh of the eight senses which we distinguished in connection with the arts. In the case of a novel or a play, we do not mind the story's falsity as history, but we do mind if it tempts us to believe that the adventures of pleasant people always have a happy ending. Similarly, it does not matter that a myth is factually untrue, but it does matter that it promises reward for the good and punishment for the wicked. If, like the religion of the older parts of the Old Testament, it leads us to expect reward and punishment in this world, then this is a false hope; if it promises them in another world, then the existence of heaven and hell becomes a question of fact, and we are back where we started, in the spiritual world which systematically eludes discovery. We cannot accept such a doctrine as poetry because regarded in this way it would be bad poetry.

But with this important class of exception, a religious or metaphysical world-picture has no point of contact with the world-picture of science. The relevant kind of criticism is to object that the implied attitude to life is self-contradictory, or does not take into account the variety of human needs, or is nourished by sensuously and emotionally impoverished images, or is 'Nay-saying', 'on the side of Death', or gives an outlet in fantasy for desires which should lead to action, or has implications for action which conflict with moral or prudential standards. Such criteria do not establish a single, true, philosophy of life. Views of life, like moral codes and works of art, may be very unlike yet equally good by necessary standards; I must choose my own by hypothetical standards, in relation to my own needs.

Linguistic philosophy does not destroy the basis of valuation; on the contrary it gives the first explanation of the relation between fact and value which can claim to be a solution and not a compromise. For any theory which assumes that assertions about God, the soul and the meaning of the universe are true in the sense that scientific propositions are true is always a compromise, a patchwork in which ideas based on scientific evidence are sewn together with others accepted because one knows by intuition that they must be true, or because moral responsibility rests on them, or life would have no significance without them, or the threatened values of the Western tradition are based on them, or out of revulsion against what a reviewer in a Sunday paper has called 'the essential vulgarity of behaviourist psychology'. However much auxiliary reasoning backs up the latter class of idea, it is always clear that the two demands which the theory seeks to reconcile are incommensurable. How heavy does scientific evidence have to be to outweigh the vulgarity of an idea or its danger to moral responsibility? How urgent must the needs of the Western tradition become before they can abolish a conflicting fact? It is time we were finished with these miserable philosophies, in which little dribbles from the world of spirit are allowed to seep through cracks in the neutral world of science, through the gaps between inorganic and organic matter and between animal and man, and into the void at the beginning in which God created the universe. We may admit that, in the words of Eliot's *Rock*, the modern world has sacrificed wisdom for knowledge, knowledge for information; but where-ever the intuitions of wisdom make contact with the observa-tions of science, wherever they can agree with or contradict them, wisdom is always vulnerable to the least particle of conflicting information.

It is an interesting paradox that a visionary such as Blake, who utterly abhors the Analytics of Bacon, Newton and Locke, does not come into collision with science although he disdains to compromise with it. At first sight the vision of the *Marriage of Heaven and Hell* seems to be absolutely opposed to the scientific world-picture. But just where is the contradiction? Blake is repelled by any account of nature which does not charge the minutest grain of sand with mystery, joy and holiness, 'melting apparent surfaces away and displaying the infinite which was hid'. However, such declarations as 'If the doors of perception were cleansed everything would appear to man as it is, infinite', 'For every thing that lives is Holy', make no contact with science. A pure description of nature is an emotional blank which we fill according to our needs and capacities, at one extreme with Blake's ecstasy, at the other with the Existentialist's feeling of the 'absurd'. The only relevant question is which response is better; and the answer is that Blake's is better, since, among other effects which are good by necessary standards, it enhances the joy of living instead of destroying it.

It may seem that we can catch Blake out in some loose thinking about 'Truth' and 'belief'; but we soon find that he uses these words consistently according to definitions of his own which have no bearing on scientific canons of proof. In his *Auguries of Innocence*,

> The bat that flits at close of eve
> Has left the brain that won't believe . . .
> If the Sun and Moon should doubt,
> They'd immediately go out,

to believe is not to assent to propositions, but to react spontaneously with joy and wonder, to doubt is to inhibit the response
by asking questions.

We seem to be nearer to a possible contradiction with
science when we read in the *Marriage of Heaven and Hell* that
'Man has no Body distinct from his Soul; for that call'd Body
is a portion of Soul discern'd by the five Senses, the chief inlets
of Soul in this age'. But it is the conception of interacting soul
and body, the impure mixture of an immaterial seat of values
known by intuition and a thing perceived by the senses, which
conflicts with behaviourism; Blake, like the behaviourists
although from different motives, denies the distinction. His
'Man has no Body distinct from his Soul' demands the same
veneration for the physical as for the spiritual; in particular, it
forbids us to deny the value of sexual appetite by separating it
from love. 'Man has no soul distinct from his body' would deny
that human behaviour is outside the scope of scientific observation, explanation and prediction. The two sentences function
differently and cannot contradict each other. If they did have
the same function, they would be equivalent, not contradictory.
('The body is soul'='The soul is body'.)

When Blake's vision does make contact with science, the
dividing line between value and fact is as plain to him as it is
to a scientist. But he approaches the line from the opposite
direction. Instead of using logical tests to exclude language
which is not descriptive, he excludes from his philosophy
language which he senses to be merely factual, emotionally
dead, and spontaneously recoils from any mixing of it with
language which is emotionally alive. He knows that a problem
is not a mystery, that mere description of a scientifically in-
explicable event such as miracle or prophecy has nothing to do
with his sense of the marvellous. A remarkable consequence is
that wherever orthodox theology has factual implications Blake
rejects them, so that his opinions on such questions seem more
scientific than those of Bacon, Newton and Locke themselves.

He is repelled by the idea of a personal God because he
feels that it is a rationalization, an abstraction from the
'Infinity in the palm of your hand'. His motive is the exact

opposite of a rationalist's, for whom God is not reasonable enough, yet the result is the same. 'The ancient Poets animated all sensible objects with Gods or Geniuses.' Later, men tried

'to realize or abstract the mental deities from their objects:
    thus began Priesthood;
Choosing forms of worship from poetic tales . . .
Thus men forgot that All deities reside in the human breast.'

He rejects miracles, prophecy, and the practical efficacy of prayer, and he assimilates prophetic to poetic inspiration:

'Isaiah answer'd: "I saw no God, nor heard any, in a finite organical perception; but my senses discovered the infinite in everything, and as I was then persuaded, and remain confirmed, that the voice of honest indignation is the voice of God, I cared not for consequences, but wrote." '

Denying Bishop Watson's contention that doubts about the Mosaic authorship of the Pentateuch do not affect its historicity, Blake comments:

'It ceases to be history and becomes a poem of probable impossibilities, fabricated for pleasure, as moderns say, but I say by inspiration . . .
'If historical facts can be written by inspiration, Milton's *Paradise Lost* is as true as Genesis or Exodus; but the evidence is nothing, for how can he who writes what he has neither seen nor heard of be an evidence of the truth of his history?'

Blake's private mythology is sometimes taken to imply a withdrawal from reality to imagination verging on insanity. But even if we ignore his insight into human motives and his concern with social and political ills, his mythology itself is evidence that his grasp of fact was surer than that of his orthodox contemporaries. He seems to live in a world different from ours; but he lives in the same world, charged

L

with an emotional significance which we lack the power to give it.

As the example of Blake implies, the present view of myth and metaphysics reverses their traditional relationship. The demand for Truth commits us to giving the place of honour to metaphysics. As soon as we are forced to admit that a myth is historically false, we assume that Truth is one stage further back, in metaphysical propositions of which the myth is a symbol. We may even congratulate ourselves on having climbed, like logicians and mathematicians, from the primitive stage of pictorial thinking to the level of pure abstraction. But we soon find ourselves in a dilemma. Sensuousness is a virtue in myth as in the arts; it may be primitive to solve questions of fact by thinking in concrete images, but abstraction diminishes the power of an emotive idea to order our responses. The more truly language seems to describe spiritual entities, the further they withdraw from sight; we are closer to 'values' in myth than in theology, in poetry than in metaphysics. The dilemma is especially acute for contemporary Christians, who have the choice between clinging to the historicity of their myths, and extracting desiccated Truths drained of the essence of their religion.

For us there is no such problem; metaphysical abstractions have the same kind of function as myth and ritual, but do not perform it as well. Symbolism has the same place in myth as in poetry. Even those who expect to detach the metaphysical kernel from a myth, and throw away the shell, know better than to think they can do this in poetry. In allegory, it is true, we must identify the ideas represented before we can understand the characters and incidents. But most poetry, when successful, burns out the intermediate ideas in the imaginative process; and if, when we finish the poem, parasitic ideas begin to breed again, we find it hard to define them clearly or agree on what they are. The meanings which a critic extracts from Yeats' Sphinx, to take an example discussed in an earlier chapter, serve only to enrich our response to the image and its context; it is the poem itself which enriches our response to life. In the *Marriage of Heaven and Hell*

The pride of the peacock is the glory of God.
The lust of the goat is the bounty of God.
The wrath of the lion is the wisdom of God.
The nakedness of woman is the work of God

is pure sensation and emotion, for Blake himself pure 'vision'.
(Cf. *A Vision of the Last Judgment:* 'Fable or allegory are a
totally distinct and inferior kind of poetry. Vision or imagination is a representation of what eternally exists, really and
unchangeably.') Since these aphorisms are not literally true,
shall we say that they illustrate the truth that God is immanent
in the universe? Blake himself seems to say as much a few
pages later, at a moment, it may be noticed, when he is
thinking and not experiencing:

'Some will say: "Is not God alone the Prolific?" I answer:
"God only Acts and Is, in existing beings or Men." '

But the answer does not differ in function from 'The pride
of the peacock is the glory of God', although its function is
much more general. It invites us to fuse our reactions to God
and to nature and man, but does not tell us how we are to
reconcile the *mysterium tremendum* with the emotions excited
by earthly things. The purpose of the four aphorisms is to
guide us towards this reconciliation; each violently juxtaposes
extremely dissimilar divine and earthly concepts, the associations of which interact and modify each other. We understand
'God is immanent' only because poets like Blake have given it
content, and 'God is transcendent' only because we have heard
God's voice through the prophets of the Old Testament and
felt the upward pull of Gothic cathedrals. Sentences of this
kind crudely manipulate complex structures of emotion and
action which more sensitive language has already articulated.

We have noticed that very different views of life may
satisfy necessary standards equally well. It follows that we can
approve a view of life without believing in it—'belief' in our
sense being, not assent to the truth of propositions, but the
disposition to behave in the way prescribed. If we take the
further step of believing, it is because we approve by hypo-

thetical standards, in relation to our own needs. It may be noticed that this is exactly how we do treat an artist's philosophy of life, a fact which has always worried people who suppose that they ought either to ignore the philosophy or judge the artist by its truth or falsehood. Faust deserves either damnation or salvation; if Marlowe's beliefs are true, must not Goethe's be false? But the reader of a poem does not, while he is reading, make the mistake of questioning the truth of any propositions on which its value seems to depend; he accepts the existence of the Devil on the same terms as the existence of Faust. What concerns him is the implicit view of life, and his valuation of this is inseparable from his valuation of the poem as a whole. If he does apply the words 'true' and 'false', he will probably, when asked to explain himself, replace them by words which refer explicitly to the poet's attitude to life— 'profound' and 'superficial', 'mature' and 'adolescent', 'balanced' and 'one-sided', 'wise' and 'silly'. He allows the conflicting beliefs of different writers to influence and contribute to the development of his own, without necessarily being converted to any one of them. But perhaps he hits on one which directly answers to his own needs; he begins to believe, to live by the writer's philosophy, and treats the book as his Bible and its story as his mythology.

According to the argument of the present essay, there are necessary and hypothetical standards by which to judge action and contemplative experience; the arts and religious and metaphysical beliefs, being instruments for living, are subject to these standards. It may be objected that this claim assimilates religion to art, and abolishes the distinction between a believing Catholic and some agnostic aesthete of the 'nineties with a taste for the vestments, dogmas and incense of the Church. But the aesthete does not believe even in our sense of the word. His assimilation of religion to art is not confined to judging it by the same standards; he responds to ritual in the same way as to art, suspending disbelief for the duration of certain exquisite experiences. If Catholic doctrine influences his conduct in the intervals, so does the paganism which he embraces while reading Catullus. It may still be objected that he cannot go further, cannot in any sense believe, unless he takes the step of assenting to the truth of dogmas. This observation is perfectly sound, but, as we have noticed already, should be turned the other way round. Judged by purely aesthetic standards, Christianity is not acceptable, because, unless a benevolent God exists, it violates fact at the one point where the arts do connect with fact. We reject works of art which nourish false expectations, which tempt us to mistake the world as it is for the world as we should like it to be. We cannot approve a novel or play which implies that the good are always rewarded and the wicked punished, nor can we, if we judge by the same standards, accept the picture of a world ruled by a benevolent God. Of course there are other standards; but unless we approve Christianity by this one, we cannot go further than respecting it as one of the great religions, cannot believe in it.

A myth of competing gods with human frailties, and of a dim Hades or Sheol occupied by the shades of good and wicked alike, is factually no truer than a myth of a single good God and a Last Judgment. But it is true to our experience that the justice of a cause has no bearing on its chances of victory. The Far Eastern philosophies, Confucianism and Taoism, also admit this simple fact; a Confucian, for example, must accept the 'decree of heaven' without expecting prosperity as the reward of right action. But the religions which originated in Western Asia, Judaism, Christianity, Zoroastrianism, Islam, all invite us to suppose that the victory of right is a matter, not of chance, but of pre-ordained law. Europeans have become so dependent on this narcotic that even rejection of Christianity does not break the habit; the doctrine of Progress and the Marxist dialectic transform the divine will into a scientific law that everything must turn out well in the end. For most Europeans, it is pessimism to recognize that good and evil have equal chances, and whoever admits the rôle of chance must endure an absurd universe. It is only in experience of the arts, in which we temporarily escape the preconceptions which rule our conduct, that we learn, through tragedy, to dispense with a universe which accords with our desires. But even tragedy, since it reconciles us specifically to evil and suffering (which may be a reason for its seeming absence outside Western literature) assumes that evil and suffering present a special problem. It is natural that sometimes I am happy, it is only my due; but why do I suffer?

We cannot, therefore, accept the Christian God as an aesthetically satisfying fiction. If we are to act on the assumption that the world is after all as we should like it to be, not as it seems to be, we need to supplement our information about the world with the further information that a benevolent God exists. How are we to prove it? Theologians of the past tried to establish that God exists by arguments which were either synthetic *a priori*, such as the proof of a First Cause and the Ontological Argument, or empirical, such as the argument from design and appeal to the historical evidence of divine intervention. Modern theologians, even when they cling to some of the arguments, give them a small place in apologetics, and are sorry that during the nineteenth century Science and Religion wasted their time fighting over such trivial, even irrelevant, issues. Yet if the existence of God is a question of fact, these are on the contrary the only relevant issues. Other considerations in favour of Christianity are at best evidence of its value as myth.

If, for example, a Christian urges me to believe, because without God life can have no meaning, or because without supernatural authority there can be no reason to obey the moral law, or because men are naturally corrupt and incapable of willing good without divine grace, or because human reason unaided by revelation is too weak to discover the Truth, or because Western civilization is rooted in the Christian religion and cannot flourish without it, then these are not reasons but motives. He is trying to undermine my resistance to intellectual temptation by offering more intellectual temptations, to stifle my suspicions that his religion is a wish-fulfilment fantasy by pointing out other wishes that it fulfils. In each case, even if we admit the premises and the terms in which he formulates them, the conclusion follows not by logic but by an emotional leap; 'If this is so, it is intolerable unless . . .' The fact, if it is a fact, that life can have no meaning without God, does not add the weight of a hair to the probability that He exists.

The Christian may also set out to persuade me of the value of his experience, and may succeed in convincing me that it is good by my own hypothetical standards and by every necessary standard except one. Here we are on quite different ground. The argument of this essay gives us no reason to doubt the value of Christian experience, nor to limit it, as old-fashioned rationalists did, to some of the moral teaching while denying it to religious devotion. Consequently a crisis of faith is not merely a conflict between reason, which is good, and emotion, which is not. The believer may be justified in his instinctive refusal to admit certain facts which can destroy his present attitude and leave him incapable of achieving another of equal quality. I have no right to criticize this subconscious choice, nor even to feel any condescension towards someone 'too weak to face the truth'. The loss involved in a little self-deception may be outweighed by a greater gain; it is a commonplace that people who accept the literal truth of a myth often live better, and even all-in-all more realistically, than sceptics who can see through it but put nothing in its place.

However, now we are back where we were. The Christian is defending, not the existence of God, but the value of an experience. He invites me to believe in a religion for the sake of its good effects, just as I suspend disbelief in a poem. But an aesthetic choice cannot conjure up a fact. In practice Christians implicitly confess that their religion is a myth, by assuming that the truth of a doctrine is the value of the motive for which it is believed, and by recognizing belief as wish-fulfilment only when its motives are bad. Thus a believer in heaven and hell will certainly despise the consoling doctrine that after death we all go to a happy country and live for eternity with our loved ones. He rejects it not because of the empirical evidence, which comes mostly from spiritualism and rather supports it, but because of the meanness of its motive, a desire to be comfortable after death whether we have earned it or not. Nineteenth-century liberalism felt the vindictive motive behind the idea of damnation, and therefore rejected it; the modern reaction scents in liberalism a fear of being held eternally responsible for one's actions, and therefore goes back to it. Both assume at bottom that the myth is true if the motives are good, false if they are bad. We are always responsible for the morals of the God in whom we choose to believe. But whether it is love or vanity which makes me trust my wife, whether my faith in the victory of a political cause is inspired by self-interest or love of humanity, whether I prefer Christianity to Islam because I feel the need of a Redeemer or, like the King choosing between the three religions, because Islam forbids me to drink wine, the worth of my motive has no bearing on the truth of my belief.

Let us conclude this chapter by glancing at the old problem of Reason vs. Intuition. The question, 'Can we establish moral, aesthetic and religious truths by rational tests, or must we depend on intuition?', is wrongly posed. There are no such truths, and therefore no intuition. We simply think, feel, want, intend, act in ways which are good or bad in relation to standards. To the extent that a man's reactions are varied, finely integrated, realistic, and otherwise right by necessary standards, we can trust his spontaneous likes and dislikes; this is all that is meant when we credit him with good taste or a sound moral sense. However, there is an important element in the intuitionist cause which is invulnerable to this criticism— the claim that we cannot discover a valid philosophy of life by analytic thought alone, and that analysis may even hinder instead of helping us. This claim seems to require a special faculty of intuition only if we overlook Ryle's distinction between 'knowing that' and 'knowing how':

A. Knowing that glass is transparent or that the earth revolves round the sun depends on observation and inference.

B. Knowing how to ride a bicycle or speak French depends on imitating others and obeying instructions, on repeating actions till practice makes perfect, on developing, by gradual maturation or by sudden leaps, the capacity to co-ordinate actions which at first have to be performed separately.

In the case of A, if we admit that there is knowledge not derived from sense-perception and inference, we do have to postulate a special faculty. If a man is seized with the conviction that his son is dead, and a minute later someone telephones to say that the son has just been killed in an accident, we must either dismiss the event as a coincidence or admit it as a case of telepathy or clairvoyance. But in the case of B, there is no place for any special faculty. To say that an acrobat has achieved by long training an intuitive knowledge of the principles of tight-rope-walking would merely obscure the fact that reasoning has entirely different functions in knowing how and knowing that. We, and the acrobat himself, know by observation and inference *that* he can walk the tightrope; but he knows without reasoning *how* to walk it, and if he were to analyse his movements while making them he would fall off.

It is easy to overlook this distinction in the case, for example, of artistic creation and appreciation. I learn how to enjoy poetry by reading and re-reading, becoming sensitive to the emotional resonance of words, developing the capacity both to unify and to diversify my response. Analysis helps, but it temporarily kills the poem, which returns to life only when I cease to analyse. For some readers, indeed, it kills the poem altogether; in reading, as in learning manual skills, many people find it hard to recover the spontaneous co-ordination of activities which they have once separated in thought. It is tempting to fall into the habit of assuming that in the un-differentiated response we enjoy an aesthetic insight into something in the poem which analysis can never discover, a value which no judgment in terms of standards can ever challenge. But even if the creation and appreciation of poetry were as spontaneous as breathing, there is no reason why the poem should not be as fully analysable in principle as the process of breathing. I cannot think out how to breathe, and trying to do so interferes with breathing; but I do not possess any information about the process which will for ever elude biologists who take to pieces the mechanism of respiration. A poet chooses a surprising word in preference to an apparent synonym, and a reader enjoys the shock of recognizing the perfectly apt word; perhaps neither can say more to justify himself than that it somehow seems richer and stronger than any alternative. If an

Empsonian critic points out that the word chosen has sub-
sidiary meanings with functions within the structure of the
poem, he is showing why it seems richer and stronger, he no
more implies that the poet consciously thought in these terms
than that the reader did. Temporarily ceasing to respond in
order to analyse, he is in the position of the tightrope-walker
recalling how he recovered his balance after a false step; the
acrobat, if of a theoretical turn of mind, can explain in
retrospect why the compensating movement kept him upright,
although if he had paused to think out which move would save
him he would have been too late to make it. A further point is
that, however little reasoning is involved in knowing *how* to do
a thing well, only reasoning can decide *that* it was done well.
Breathing and acrobatics are equally spontaneous whether
they are going well or badly, and only observation and
inference can establish the difference. Too little oxygen is
reaching my lungs, therefore my breathing is out of order; the
acrobat fell off the rope, therefore his move was the wrong one.

No one is converted to a way of life by reason alone; in this
respect the rationalist differs from the intuitionist only in
being troubled by his inconsistency, and perhaps hiding it from
himself. Comparing another way of life with my own, I may
judge that by necessary standards it is better than my own,
more consistent, more adequate to the believer's ends, more
compatible with fact. (As we have seen, the last condition
implies, not that religious and metaphysical tenets should be
factual, but that any presuppositions which are factual should
be true.) Yet this better way of life remains wrong for me unless
I share its ends, and no further reasoning can convert me to it
without a spontaneous change in my own ends. Suppose that
I find my life purposeless, and look for salvation in Christianity
or Communism. Having convinced myself that Thomist or
Marxist theology is rationally cogent, I try to act as religious or
revolutionary duty requires. Since each of these systems dis-
guises the hypothetical character of its imperatives, I seem now
to have a purpose in life fully supported by reason. Yet somehow all I have is a set of excrescent religious or political
opinions, for the sake of which I deny myself what in fact I

want; I still lack the gift of faith, still understand only in theory the Unity of Theory and Practice. It is only when I begin to desire spontaneously to serve God or the revolutionary cause, and all other desires fall into a new pattern, that I learn how to become a Christian or a Communist.

Learning how to think, feel and act in a new way, through slow maturation or a sudden reorientation, is not a rational process; but it is only by applying rational tests that we can learn whether the change is for better or for worse. It is in the spontaneous leap from an inferior to a better organization, in moments of aesthetic or religious illumination, that we seem to enjoy insight into values; and if we are misled by this metaphor 'insight', it is natural to suppose that we have grasped without thought truths irrefutable by thought. It is equally natural that rationalists who reject these truths, offered to them as knowledge *that*, should overlook the possibility of advance in knowing *how*. But both points of view are as inadequate as the pre-Freudian assumption that the visions of seers are either perceptions of another world or delusions which prove their insanity. We must regard the metaphysical discoveries of intuition in the way that psychologists regard dreams and visions, as symptoms of involuntary changes, for the better or for the worse—remembering that the psychologist's diagnosis assumes objective tests of mental health.

13

MYSTICISM

'Nothing in the world is bigger than the tip of a hair, and Mount T'ai is small; no one lives longer than a child dead in its swaddling clothes, and P'eng-tsu[1] died young; heaven and earth were born together with me, and I am one with all things.' Chuang-tzŭ, ch. 2.

'You never enjoy the world aright, till the Sea itself floweth in your veins, till you are clothed with the heavens, and crowned with the stars: and perceive yourself to be the sole heir of the whole world, and more than so, because men are in it who are every one sole heirs as well as you.'

Traherne, *Centuries of Meditation*, 1st century, no. 29.

WHAT are the Taoist Chuang-tzŭ and the Christian Traherne telling us? A common answer would be that they present, embedded in poetic metaphors from which we can easily detach it, certain information unknown to science. All things are one, and each of us is the universe. Defenders and critics of the mystical experience alike argue in terms of the truth or falsehood of such claims as that the distinctions between self and other, good and evil, are illusory, that behind the multiplicity of the world perceived by the senses there is the One, pure Being, the indivisible Reality, experienced in mystical illumination. Positivists object that there is no means of testing such assertions; therefore they cannot be meaningful, let alone true; therefore the experience is a delusion. Mystics reply that if science cannot verify their claims, so much the worse for science; theirs is a higher kind of knowledge, discovered by an intuition superior to reason and perception. Underlying both

[1] The Chinese Methuselah.

arguments is the assumption that the utterances of mystics are either true or worthless, an assumption which is no longer tenable now that we have begun to recognize the variety of functions which language performs. 'All things are one', I shall argue, does not describe the world, but recommends a way of dealing with the world. Mystics do not give us information which scientists cannot discover, and whenever they speak of Truth, Being and Reality, whenever they present their recommendations in the disguise of descriptive statements, they are invading territory from which rationalists have both the right and the might to expel them. However, reclassifying the sentence does not discredit it as meaningless, but alters the kind of test which applies to it. What matters is not the truth of any supposed information, but the value of a way of living.

The mystic claims a special access to reality which the rest of us do not share. Why should you take it for granted, he asks, that reason and sense-perception are the only sources of knowledge? It may be inconvenient that some have private sources unavailable to the rest, and no doubt it is wise to treat their claims, too easily abused, with some caution; but has not experiment already gone a long way towards proving the reality of telepathy and clairvoyance? Knowing that you cannot describe colours to a man born blind, should you not have the humility to admit that others may see what they cannot describe to you? It may be objected that mystics disagree to a much greater extent than ordinary people disagree about the data of sense-perception. But in fact mystics agree to an extent which it is difficult to laugh off; the doctrine that 'All things are one', although not universal, is predominant in India and the Far East, and appears with remarkable frequency, as heresy or as metaphor verging on heresy, even in Christian and Muslim mysticism, where its implication that the One transcends the distinctions between personal and impersonal, self and God, good and evil, clashes with the orthodox belief in a personal and ethical deity. I cannot describe a colour to you, only point it out—unless you are blind. Similarly I cannot describe what I see in ecstasy, but I can teach you techniques of meditation by which to see it yourself. Of course, you may still be blind; mystical insight is like aesthetic insight, some people have it and some have not. But until you have tried, is it not presumptuous to say that the truth which it reveals is delusion?

However, the analogy between mystical insight and a sixth sense does not stand up to examination. Admittedly I cannot describe colours to a man born blind. But he can confirm that the information 'I live in the house with the red door' helps people to pick out his house from others. The blind man knows that others possess a sense which he lacks, because they find their way about more easily than he does, and notice things and events before his own senses perceive them. People with normal senses test claims to extra-sensory perception in the same way, for example by card-guessing experiments. More-over, tests by other senses are necessary to the possessors of special faculties as well as to doubting witnesses. A telepathist may have hunches and premonitions accompanied by a strong feeling of subjective conviction, but he has no reason to heed them unless the evidence of his other senses has confirmed similar hunches in the past. Any vision may be a hallucination; in order to confirm that we are not imagining but perceiving, we must compare it with other perceptions, our own and other people's. If there is no means of verifying by other senses the existence of an object experienced, then it is meaningless to postulate such an object in addition to the experience. Let us suppose that someone were to claim that in dreams we witness real events occurring on the other side of the moon. This claim would be testable; even without waiting for the reports of space travellers, we could object that the moon's atmosphere cannot support the human beings we see in dreams. On the other hand, if it were maintained that the events occur, not on the moon, but on a different plane of reality accessible only through dreams, and that they have no effects on the reality perceived by the senses, we should at once recognize that the claim is meaningless.

But the mystic claims to experience in ecstasy a Reality to which there is no access except through ecstasy. He enjoys an intense subjective conviction of the value of the experience, and perhaps satisfies us that it has made him a better and happier man; but these are signs of the value of the experience, not of the truth of the vision. The mystic himself has no means of testing the truth of any information he brings us. Even for himself, the experience and the subjective conviction can establish nothing; they merely put him in the position of a telepathist who has no means of testing his own hunches. The objection is a logical one, which we can raise without having shared the mystic's vision, just as a man who had never dreamed in his life could raise it against the claim that we dream of events on another plane of reality.

The agreement of so many mystics about the nature of Reality also proves nothing. Although there are many mystics, especially Christians and Muslims, who do not report that everything is one, there is certainly enough agreement on this point to suggest a connection between the experience and the assertion. But if victims of the same drug or mental disorder share the same kinds of delusion, we conclude, not that there must be something in their delusions, but that the same causes have the same effects on thought and vision. There is a large measure of agreement among paranoiacs that they are men of unrecognized greatness suffering persecution. In this case the agreement is accompanied by disagreement as to who is the noble victim of persecution, so that we are not impressed; and the paranoiac makes factual statements which we can check. But he can justly claim that if we were not deaf to the voices which speak to him we should recognize the truth of his assertions; for if we did hear them we too should be paranoiac. We do not confirm the vision by sharing it; it is because we do not share it that we are able to judge it by objective tests.

Suppose that my friend, who is several drinks ahead of me, insists that things are really double, and that their appearance of singleness while we are sober is a delusion. If I object that they still look single to me, he can easily teach me to see things as they really are—have another drink. In this case I have an objective test even when drunk; I manipulate things more successfully when I see them as single. The mystic's subjective conviction is not confirmed by the frequency with which others who undergo the same training come to share it, since any delusion is shared by whoever submits to the conditions which produce the delusion. There is an embarrassingly large measure of agreement among mystics that at a certain point in their development they achieve magic powers. If we put this conviction on the same level as paranoiac and alcoholic delusions, may we not treat their metaphysical claims in the same way?

It is well known that mescalin and nitrous oxide may induce unusual experiences accompanied by an intense subjective feeling of significance and a conviction that 'All things are one.' But it is extremely implausible to suggest that drugs which distort our vision of commonplace reality can introduce us to a deeper reality. If a man intoxicated with mescal is liable to believe that his limbs are changing in length and shape and that he can knead metal with his hands, are we to suppose that certain of his visions are not less but more dependable than everyday vision, merely on the grounds that he enjoys an intense conviction of value and significance? It must be added, however, that if we clearly distinguish between the truth of his metaphysical claims and the value of his experience, such considerations affect the former only. I cannot discredit the value of cheerfulness, confidence and generosity by pointing out that alcohol temporarily induces these states in normally gloomy, bashful and stingy people. I can object only that drinking is the wrong way to win a lasting self-confidence or happiness, since the effect soon wears off. Defenders of mysticism take a similar view of mescalin, quite justly if the question of truth is left out of account. They assume that, although the mescalin-taker's conviction of the value of his experience is not deceptive, he must disdain such short cuts if he is to achieve a vision which is more than a tantalizing glimpse, an ecstasy which will radically and permanently alter his view of life.

The mystic's insights are ineffable; this is a point on which defenders and enemies of mysticism find it expedient to agree. For the former it is an excuse to withdraw beyond the reach of rational criticism, for the latter a confession that mystics have nothing meaningful to say. Both sides tend to play down the fact that mystics do succeed in communicating something of what their experience is like. They communicate, however, as poets and not as philosophers, at once emotionally lucid and intellectually obscure. Those who, like myself, have never enjoyed such experiences, have at least an inkling of what mystics are talking about; otherwise who would be persuaded to aim at a goal which he could not even conceive? The mystic is intelligible to the unmystical to the extent that he is a poet; only the type of abstract thinker who is insensitive to the subtler emotive functions of language has no idea what mystics are getting at.

'This earth is the honey of all beings; all beings the honey of this earth. The bright eternal Self that is in earth, the bright eternal Self that lives in this body, are one and the same; that is immortality, that is Spirit, that is all.

Water is the honey of all beings; all beings the honey of water. The bright eternal Self that is in water, the bright eternal Self that lives in human seed, are one and the same; that is immortality, that is Spirit, that is all.

Wind is the honey of all beings; all beings the honey of wind. The bright eternal Self that is in wind, the bright eternal Self that lives in breath, are one and the same; that is immortality, that is Spirit, that is all.

The sun is the honey of all beings; all beings the honey of the sun. The bright eternal Self that is in the sun, the bright eternal Self that lives in the eye, are one and the same; that is immortality, that is Spirit, that is all.

The moon is the honey of all beings; all beings the honey of the moon. The bright eternal Self that is in the moon, the bright eternal Self that lives in the mind, are one and the same; that is immortality, that is Spirit, that is all.

Thunder is the honey of all beings; all beings the honey of

M

thunder. The bright eternal Self that is in thunder, the bright eternal Self that lives in the voice, are one and the same; that is immortality, that is Spirit, that is all.

Self is the honey of all beings; all beings the honey of Self. The bright eternal Self that is everywhere, the bright eternal Self that lives in a man, are one and the same; that is immortality, that is Spirit, that is all.'[1]

It is easy to see why the abstract statement of the last stanza is so much more effective as the culmination of this tremendous nonsense than it would be in a context of philosophical analysis. The passage works on us through comparisons which are, not analogies from which to infer, but poetic similes; hypnotized by the unrelenting repetition of a single rhythmic pattern, we feel the breath merge into the wind, the eye into the sun, the voice into thunder. As another example we might take this stanza of St. John of the Cross;

> Oh noche, que guiaste,
> oh noche amable mas que el alborada,
> oh noche, que juntaste
> Amado con amada,
> amada en el Amado trasformada!

('O night which guided me, O night lovelier than the dawn, O night which joined Lover with mistress, mistress transformed into the Lover!')

Here the comparison of God and the soul with lover and mistress is not an analogy which clarifies a relationship hard to understand in the abstract; it directly evokes a passionate delight in union with God like that of a woman possessed by her lover, and it makes us feel the union more vividly (not conceive it more clearly) by fusing the sounds of the words Lover and mistress by assonance and alliteration—'*amada en*

[1] Brihadaranyaka-Upanishad (seven of fourteen stanzas, including the first and last) in *The Ten Principal Upanishads*, translated by Shri Purohit Swami and W. B. Yeats (London 1937), pp. 133-5.

el Amado trasformada'. We are nearest to the mystic's Truth when we let him intoxicate us by rhythm, stun us by repetitions, deceive us by the sleight-of-hand of assonance and alliteration. To be understood, he must use language as though it were mescalin.

This may seem to be labouring a point which a defender of mysticism will freely concede. 'You are merely showing the limitations of your abstract intellect,' he may reply. 'Of course there is a higher kind of Truth which only poetry can communicate.' But this answer sacrifices the claim that only those who have shared the mystic's experience have the right to judge his reports; for it puts the truth of mysticism on the same level as truth in the arts, which is a matter on which many more people are competent to form opinions. X says that Beethoven's last Quartets express a vision of ultimate Truth, an insight into the deepest Reality; Y is content to say that they express a mood of serenity, mystery and reconciliation which has permanently affected his attitude to life. X perhaps suspects that Y is too coarse-grained to understand him. But the chances are that Y does know what X means, just as he would if X were to insist that he can see that the world is flat, or hear that foreigners have an accent while we have none, or perceive by introspection a mind distinct from his body. These are all interpretations which, for anyone who has not reached a certain level of self-consciousness, seem not to be interpretations at all, but direct reports of the evidence of experience. If mystics use the words Truth and Reality as X uses them, we have all the more reason to dismiss their metaphysical claims. But we also have reason to give mystical experience the same respect as aesthetic experiences which, without conveying any new information, make us respond differently to what we already know.

How then are we to regard the claim that 'All things are one'? A sentence of the form 'X is one' functions quite differently from the formula 'There is one X'. The latter is a factual statement, verified by counting. 'X is one', on the other hand, is a maxim forbidding us to do something to a part without doing the same to the rest. We may count a collection

of trees as one forest, or a thousand trees, or half the available
supply of timber, but it would be meaningless to ask whether
the forest is really one, many or a part. The owner might, however, say 'The forest is one'; he would be expressing a decision
not to divide it, a warning that anyone who tries to buy part of
it is wasting his time. The formula 'X is one' is often justified
by showing that the parts are interrelated to such a degree that
any attempt to do something to an isolated part must be
unsuccessful. When we use this kind of argument, we tend to
speak as though 'X is one' were a factual statement equivalent
to 'The parts of X are interdependent'; but the interdependence
is a matter of degree, and what degree we find relevant depends
on the course of action we are considering. 'France and Algeria
are one' and 'Goa is an integral part of Portugal' are warnings
to Algerians and Goanese not to seek political independence.
You can justify the warnings, should you be so inclined, by
arguing that the economic and cultural interests of these
peoples are so closely interwoven with those of the colonial
power that separation would injure both sides. If a psychologist declares that 'The mind is one', he is advising us not to
study mental activities in isolation from each other. He may
admit that the study of isolated parts has been fruitful in the
past, but holds that its possibilities were already exhausted
when the Gestalt school appeared, and that the division of the
mind into the separate compartments of thinking, feeling and
striving is now a hindrance to further advance.

    'All things are one' is therefore not a descriptive statement.
It bears a certain resemblance to such phrases as 'It is all one',
'It is all the same to me', which express a lack of preference
for one course rather than another. We might use it to convey
a total apathy in a meaningless universe; indeed, this becomes
its significance for Mrs. Moore in E. M. Forster's *Passage to
India*. Obviously it has another significance for mystics, whose
goal is not apathy but bliss. However, if we ask a defender of
mysticism what difference it makes to believe that all things
are one, he will freely admit that it does not help him to discover information about the world, as 'The mind is one'
helped the Gestalt psychologists; the difference is that the man

who is conscious of his unity with all things is finally rid of
desire, ceases to prefer joy to misery, good to evil, life to death,
himself to others, accepts everything and excludes nothing, is
totally reconciled to all that is. We must conclude, then, that
'All things are one', instead of describing things, prescribes an
altered relationship with things. It does not state a truth which
Chuang-tzǔ, Traherne, the *Upanishads* and St. John of the
Cross adorn with poetic embroidery; it is itself desiccated
poetry which evokes vaguely and generally an attitude which
the rhythm and metaphor of mystical poetry begins to define
and which techniques of meditation develop further. For those
of us who have neither the temperament nor the training for
mysticism, it is far from clear what this attitude is like; but
we can take the mystic's word for it that he does know what
it is like. We cannot trust the metaphysical conclusions which
he draws from his experience, but we can take his word for the
experience itself.

If we mistake 'All things are one' for a descriptive statement, we are tempted to defend or criticize mysticism with the
wrong kind of arguments. When mystics are not philoso-
phizing, they recognize quite plainly that a mystical principle
is merely a guide directing us towards an experience, acting, to
quote some Zen similes, as a finger pointing at the moon, a
boat to be discarded once you are across the water, a com-
mentary on the sudden cry 'Ah, this!' in the moment of
illumination. But when they do philosophize, they argue as
though the principle conveys information about the constitu-
tion of the universe, information which we can understand
and confirm by *a priori* reasoning, even without sharing the
experience. Thus Neo-Platonists try to convince us, for example,
that since an army ceases to be an army when it loses its unity,
we can say that a thing is what it is only as long as it is one;
therefore everything depends for its being on possession of the
One. They offer us bad logic instead of good poetry, and make
it difficult to penetrate through the metaphysical rubbish to the
experience beneath. On the other hand, positivists imagine
that they can refute mysticism by showing that its principles
are not factual statements, and that the parasitic arguments

which breed on them are nonsense. Of course 'All things are one' is unverifiable by sense experience, neither true nor false, meaningless according to the definition used by Logical Positivists. But 'Press Button A' and 'Take the second turning on the left' are also neither true nor false, and are none the worse for that. It is absurd to suppose that 'All things are one' can be discredited by shifting it from one pigeon-hole to another, and showing that instead of conveying a fact it merely points the way to perfect happiness. 'Take the second turning on the left' proves to be sound advice if you do reach your destination; the test of a mystical system is whether it does lead those who practise it to the reconciliation with all things which mystics promise.

A mystical doctrine is not a system of vague ideas, to be learned by reading the *Enneads* or the *Upanishads*; it is a system of precise instructions, from teacher to disciple, as to how to sit down, breathe, meditate. Zen Buddhism, for example, is not a philosophy but a monastic discipline, a technique of meditation, an artistic tradition, a ritual of serving tea; outside this context, which exists only in Japan, there is little a Westerner can get from books except shaggy-dog stories about patriarchs of the T'ang dynasty, and some mistransmitted emotions which are said to go very well with cool jazz and marijuana. Anyone who wishes to test the value of mysticism needs to practise its techniques under a qualified guru, instead of looking for reasons for and against its metaphysical claims. Those of us with an unpromising temperament cannot evaluate the mystic's way of life, any more than we can judge a poem without reading it, or without being able to respond to it. Although, as we have seen, this spiritual insensibility does not disqualify us for arguing with mystics over metaphysical questions, it does prevent us from valuing their experience. We can judge only the experiences which mystics succeed in evoking in us through poetry, and the effects of mysticism on the personalities of those who practise it. If we find these good by aesthetic and moral standards, we have a reason for exploring further. We can dismiss all questions of truth and falsehood; the mystic's conviction that he is one with the universe is of a different order from believing, say, that he has the power of levitation, and cannot be a delusion, any more than it can be true, since it has no bearing either way on verifiable facts. What matters is whether an attitude of all-embracing acceptance is psychologically possible, whether we can attain it ourselves, whether it is good or bad. It is at least plausible to object that it is bad to look on good and evil with the same serenity; one ought not to be reconciled to human misery and injustice, one should try to change them. This may be an unsound criticism, but it is the right kind of criticism.

14

CONCLUSION

I HAVE not answered the opening question of this essay, 'By what standards shall I live?' My task has been linguistic analysis, the clarification of the types of reasoning by which each of us seeks his own answer. Linguistic analysis distinguishes between necessary and hypothetical standards, shows that the former have no practical application unless combined with the latter, seeks proofs of the former and criteria by which to test the latter. This kind of philosophy has been called 'the grammar of science'; it is also the grammar of morals, poetry and myth.

The linguistic philosopher in his professional capacity is, and should be, a rather dull creature, a despised but useful servant of scientists, moralists, poets and visionaries. His task is to show his masters how they are using words, how to test and co-ordinate their arguments, whether they are talking nonsense, whether they are contradicting each other. It is now the practice in England to confine the name 'philosophy' to this discipline. One may well prefer, remembering that etymologically philosophy is the 'love of wisdom', to reserve it instead for thinkers who do attempt to answer the question, 'How shall I live?' Linguistic analysts cannot usurp the place of such thinkers, but they can point out to them that their work is subject to the same standards as the arts, and that whenever they try to argue like logicians or scientists they are confusing the issue. Since Kierkegaard and Nietzsche such philosophers have indeed generally been artists. Like other artists they resent critics, most of all trivial, hair-splitting, insensitive critics who systematically avoid all really serious questions. But if the linguistic philosopher has a soul, he has no right to show it.

For linguistic analysts there are no profound questions, no mysteries. Mysteries belong to the other kind of philosopher, who at once exposes himself to the analyst's criticism if he makes the mistake of proposing rational solutions. We must rid ourselves of the impure fascination of riddles like the ancient puzzle of Infinity. Is it a problem or a mystery? If it is a problem, we need an emotionally arid solution which dispels the fascination. If it is like the *kōans* of Zen Buddhism ('What is the sound of one hand clapping?'), we are not seeking a logical solution at all; we want the tension of the paradox to burst the rational control which inhibits a spontaneous inward reorientation. But we confound two different purposes, and refuse to be satisfied either by a logical solution, which seems to be a superficial answer to a profound question, or by an ecstatic cry of 'Katsu!', which seems to be no answer at all.

SHORT READING LIST

Logical Positivism and Linguistic Philosophy

Ludwig Wittgenstein, *Tractatus Logico-Philosophicus* (1922); *Philosophical Investigations* (1953)

A. J. Ayer, *Language, Truth and Logic* (1936)

Gilbert Ryle, *The Concept of Mind* (1949)

J. O. Urmson, *Philosophical Analysis* (1956)

David Pole. *The Later Philosophy of Wittgenstein* (1958)

The following are criticisms of Linguistic Philosophy:

G. R. G. Mure, *Retreat from Truth* (1958)

Ernest Gellner, *Words and Things* (1959)

The Language of Morals

G. E. Moore, *Principia Ethica* (1903)

The following approach morals from the viewpoint of Linguistic Philosophy:

Charles L. Stevenson, *Ethics and Language* (1945)

Stephen Toulmin, *The Place of Reason in Ethics* (1950)

R. M. Hare, *The Language of Morals* (1952)

P. H. Nowell-Smith, *Ethics* (1954)

A. N. Prior, *Logic and the Basis of Ethics* (1956)

Stuart Hampshire, *Thought and Action* (1959)

C. K. Ogden and I. A. Richards, *Meaning of Meaning* (1923)

T. E. Hulme, *Speculations* (1924)

I. A. Richards, *Principles of Literary Criticism* (1924); *Science and Poetry* (1926); *Coleridge on Imagination* (1934)

William Empson, *Seven Types of Ambiguity* (1930); *Structure of Complex Words* (1951)

INDEX